Cooking
with
Rachel

Cooking with Rachel

Creative Vegetarian and Macrobiotic Cuisine

by Rachel Albert

edited by Laurel Ruggles

George Ohsawa Macrobiotic Foundation
Oroville, California

Illustrations by Sheri Peterson
Cover design by Carl Campbell

First edition 1989

Library of Congress Catalog Card Number: 89-85012
ISBN 0-918860-49-0

☰ *Foreword*

For many years we have recognized food as a symbol of good living, ethnic origin, pleasure, and beauty. Cooking is considered an art and many families and countries pride themselves on their culinary expertise.

Food and cooking have been used to attract people, make friends, and to share love. A meal is more than just a group of nutrients on a plate to satisfy our physical being; it is the way we communicate with others, how we transform the basic foods into something beautiful that feeds many aspects of our existence.

This, the second book that Rachel Albert has written, is full of enticing, delicious, and lovingly-created recipes. I have had an opportunity to taste most of her creations and recommend them for an adventure into natural culinary art.

Enjoy,

Jorge Badillo-Cochran, N. D.

☰ *Preface*

The importance of good eating has been recognized for many years as one of the cornerstones of better health.

In the last twenty years information, products, and exercise programs to enhance health have multiplied. Many people are concerned with obtaining unadulterated products and avoiding chemicals added to foods during growth or processing. We are entering a time when people want to know more about how to prevent health problems and are willing to expend whatever effort is necessary to maintain health. It makes sense.

Many years ago Hippocrates, the father of medicine, taught that we should let food be our medicine. Now we are finally recognizing that we need to understand more about food to know more about ourselves.

Jorge Badillo-Cochran, N. D.

☰ *Introduction*

This book is a compilation of recipes which appeal to a wide range of tastes and food preferences. While some of these recipes are strictly macrobiotic, others are intended to be used as fun foods, party foods, and transitional foods. My purpose in writing this book has been to share new recipes, many of which people suggested or had cravings for, as well as to include many favorite recipes from my first book *Gourmet Whole Foods*, no longer in print. And, I wanted to make adaptations of American and ethnic favorites that are like your old favorites but with higher-quality, lower-fat ingredients and without meat, sugar, or dairy products.

For some people these recipes may need to be adjusted. If you have a special dietary need or health condition you may have to skip over certain recipes. The purpose of having healing foods and fun foods in one volume is primarily to lend variety and inspiration to the experience of cooking, presenting, and enjoying the foods that are available within a broad macrobiotic framework. It is hoped that you will share these recipes and dishes with your family and friends, many of whom may not be macrobiotic but will likely enjoy these richer dishes and be inspired to try cooking with some of these new ingredients. It is much easier for people to make the transition to a macrobiotic or whole-foods diet when they are able to see, taste, and create dishes that are familiar to them and are similar to foods which they have enjoyed in the past.

The macrobiotic diet offers a wide array of tastes, textures, colors, and foods. This can be overwhelming to newcomers and can be a stumbling block to people who don't know what to do when they remove meat, sugar, eggs, dairy foods, and pre-packaged, processed foods from their diets. Most people don't realize how wide a selection of foods is available beyond the standard American diet.

This book will show you how to make healthier sandwiches, grain, noodle, or vegetable salads, casseroles, soups, stews, cookies, cakes, pancakes, puddings, pates, dips, snack foods, party foods, and ethnic favorites. This can make the journey to a healthier diet less rocky and overwhelming, and can make it easier to share your new way of eating with friends and family.

In my experiences teaching cooking classes, giving macrobiotic dinners, operating a restaurant, catering, and doing cooking demonstrations, bridging the gap between the standard American diet and macrobiotics has been facilitated by cooking a slightly wider macrobiotic diet and by making more familiar foods and dishes with macrobiotic quality ingredients. In this way we can make macrobiotics more accessible and less intimidating to the curious onlooker, friend, or family member.

Rachel Albert

Contents

Soups and Salads

Soups

Azuki Bean and Onion Soup

1 cup azuki beans
4 cups water or stock
6-inch piece kombu
1 or 2 carrots, cubed or ½ to 1 cup pumpkin, cubed
1 onion, chopped
2 to 3 Tbsp. shoyu
ginger root, grated and squeezed

Soak beans 5 to 6 hours or overnight in water. Discard soak water; add 4 cups fresh water or stock and kombu. Cover and boil several hours or pressure cook for 30 minutes. Add vegetables and shoyu; boil or pressure cook until vegetables are tender. Add more liquid as necessary. Add ginger juice to taste and remove from heat. Puree azukis and cooked vegetables in a food mill or press through a strainer to make a creamy soup.

Black Soybean Soup

2 cups black soybeans
¼ tsp. sea salt
6-inch piece kombu
water
1 to 2 large white onions, cut in crescents
stalks from broccoli and cauliflower, cut finely
4 to 5 cups water or stock
1 to 2 tsp. shoyu
½ to 1 Tbsp. light yellow or barley miso
ginger root, grated and squeezed
1 handful fresh parsley, chopped

Soak soybeans overnight in salted water. Drain beans. Pour beans in a large pot. Add kombu and fresh water or stock to cover beans 1 to 2 inches. Bring to a boil, then shock with ⅓ cup cold water. Repeat shock treatment once, then reduce heat to low and simmer, covered, 2½ to 3 hours. Periodically add more cold water, as this helps make the beans sweeter and cook better. Beans should be soft enough to chew, but not mushy.

When beans are tender, add onions and broccoli or cauliflower stalks. Bring to a boil, then add shoyu. Simmer over low heat 30 to 40 minutes or until vegetables are soft. Season with miso; adjust amount to taste. The soup should be sweet, not overly salty. Simmer 4 to 5 minutes. Add ginger juice to taste. Garnish with fresh chopped parsley.

Serving Suggestions:
– Serve with brown rice, rice and barley, or rice with hato mugi barley, baked, boiled, or nishime-cooked squash, and boiled salad or greens with seed dressing.

Bok Choy Saute Soup

5 shiitake mushrooms
¼ cup wakame
water for soaking mushrooms and wakame
5 cups water or soup stock
1 cup fresh daikon, cut in thin quarter moons
2 Tbsp. barley miso
sesame oil
3 cups finely cut bok choy
fresh parsley or scallions, chopped (optional)

Soak shiitake in water to cover for 1 hour. Soak wakame in water to cover for 20 to 30 minutes. Save soak water from mushrooms and wakame and add water or stock to measure 5 cups.

Cut wakame finely and add to pot of stock. Slice mushrooms finely and add to stock. Cover and bring to a boil, then reduce heat to low. Simmer 15 minutes. Add daikon and simmer 5 to 6 minutes.

Remove 1 cup of stock and dissolve miso in it. Add back to pot. Add more dissolved miso if desired. Simmer 4 to 5 minutes, but do not boil.

Brush a cast iron skillet with a few drops of sesame oil and saute bok choy 2 to 3 minutes. Add bok choy to soup and serve garnished with chopped scallions or fresh parsley, if desired.

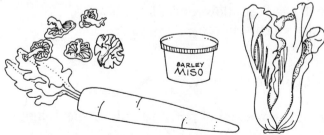

Cream of Carrot Soup Concentrate

8 cups cut carrots
4 cups water
5-inch piece kombu
miso

To make soup concentrate, pressure cook carrots with water and kombu 15 to 20 minutes. Remove kombu and set it aside to cook with beans or other vegetables. Puree carrots and store in jars in refrigerator. Concentrate will keep for up to one week.

To make soup, dilute concentrate with an equal amount of water, and heat. Dissolve barley miso or chickpea miso in a small amount of soup, allowing ½ teaspoon miso per cup of soup or to taste. Add to soup and simmer 3 more minutes.

Garnish each serving with a dash of green ao-nori flakes and/or a teaspoon or two of grated daikon radish.

Cauliflower and Pea Soup

1 handful wakame, crumbled, or soaked and chopped
1 large onion, cut in crescents
2 to 3 stalks celery, chopped
2 to 3 carrots, cut finely
1 small head cauliflower or ¾ large head
1½ cups green split peas
8 cups water
4 tsp. light or white miso
½ to ¾ cup fresh parsley, chopped

Place wakame in bottom of pot; add onion, celery, and carrots. Cut cauliflower florets from stem, then cut stem, core, and greens finely. Add to other vegetables. Rinse split peas in colander or sieve. Add to vegetables with water.

Bring to a boil, then lower heat and simmer, covered, for 45 to 50 minutes. Puree in a food mill or mash through a metal sieve with a large spoon. Return puree to the pot and bring to a boil. Dissolve miso in a small amount of puree and add to soup. Add parsley. Simmer for 4 to 5 minutes but do not boil.

Serving Suggestions:

- Serve with pressure-cooked brown rice, sauteed, blanched, or steamed greens, cooked squash or parsnips, and dry-roasted pumpkin seeds or sunflower seeds.

- This soup keeps for up to a week in the refrigerator and is easy to reheat for a quick lunch with a small loaf of sourdough whole grain bread and a fresh salad or lightly cooked vegetables.

- Make an aspic: Add more water to soup, and more seasoning if desired. Soak agar agar flakes in 1 to 2 cups cold water; 1 tablespoon agar agar per 1 cup soup. Add to soup, bring to a boil, then cook over low heat 10 minutes to dissolve agar flakes. Pour into mold and let it gel. Cut and serve.

Chickpea and Squash Bisque

2 to 3 cups dry chickpeas
6 to 9 cups water
6-inch piece kombu
water to cover
½ kabocha squash or 2 small buttercup squash
1 large onion
3 cups water or stock
1 to 2½ Tbsp. white miso

Soak chickpeas overnight in 3 times as much water as beans. Drain. Place beans and kombu in a pressure cooker. Add fresh water to cover beans by 1½ inches. Pressure cook 1 hour or until beans are tender.

Scrub squash and cut in cubes, removing seeds but leaving the skin on the squash. Cut onion finely in crescents. Add squash and onions to beans with about 3 cups water or other liquid. Do not stir. Bring to a boil, then simmer, covered, over low heat 35 to 55 minutes or until vegetables are soft.

Press beans and vegetables through a strainer using a large wooden spoon or puree in a food mill. Dissolve miso in a small amount of the puree or hot water and add back to mixture. Simmer 3 minutes but do not boil.

Leftovers may be served chilled or reheated.

Corn Onion Soup

- 5 cups water or stock
- 4 large white onions, cut finely in crescents
- corn from 4 ears fresh corn
- 1 to 3 Tbsp. white or yellow miso
- minced scallion
- green nori flakes or toasted nori

Boil water and cook onions over medium heat 30 to 35 minutes. Add corn kernels and cook 20 minutes.

Dissolve miso in a bowl of hot soup liquid. Add back to pot and simmer 3 minutes. Garnish each serving with scallion or nori.

Dried Daikon Soup with Parsley and Onion

- 4 cups water
- ½ cup dried daikon
- 6-inch piece kombu
- sesame oil
- 1 large onion, cut in crescents
- ½ to 1 tsp. miso per cup soup
- chopped parsley (optional)

Boil 1 cup of the water, add daikon and soak for 1 hour. Soak kombu in 3 cups cold water for 20 to 30 minutes then cut into fine pieces. Place dried daikon, kombu, and all soaking water in a pot.

Brush a skillet with sesame oil. Saute onion over medium heat until translucent. Add onion to soup pot and simmer, covered, 15 to 20 minutes. Add more water if soup is too thick.

Remove about a cup of soup broth and dissolve miso in it. Add this back to the soup and simmer without boiling 4 to 5 minutes. Serve garnished with parsley.

Daikon, Onion, and Wakame Miso Soup

6 cups water or stock
1 large onion, cut finely in crescents (approximately 3½ cups)
3 cups daikon radish, finely cut in quarter moons
¼ cup wakame, crumbled, or soaked and chopped
1 to 2 Tbsp. miso, or to taste
½ lemon, cut in thin slices
2 to 3 scallions, cut finely

Bring water to a boil. Add onions, daikon, and wakame and simmer, covered, 30 minutes or until vegetables are tender.

Dissolve miso in a small amount of soup stock. Add it back to pot and simmer 3 to 4 minutes; do not boil. Garnish each serving with a lemon slice and scallions. Serves 6 to 8.

Variation:

– Grate 1 tablespoon fresh ginger and squeeze ginger in your fist. Add the juice to the soup just before serving.

Daikon, Carrot, and Wakame Miso Stew

1 to 2 handfuls wakame, crumbled, or soaked and chopped
5 to 6 cups water or stock
1 large onion or 2 medium onions, cut in crescents
3 carrots, cut in irregular wedges
daikon radish, cut in wedges, an equivalent amount as for
   carrots
1 to 2 Tbsp. miso
chopped scallions

Place wakame, water, onion, carrots, and daikon in a pot. Bring to a boil, then reduce heat and simmer, covered, for 30 minutes or until vegetables are tender. Add more water if needed to make a thick, chunky stew. The broth will be very sweet.

Remove a small bowl of broth, then dissolve miso in it and add back to the stew. Simmer over low heat for 3 minutes, then serve garnished with chopped scallions.

Variations:

– Add juice from grated ginger root just before serving. To obtain juice, grate a tablespoon of fresh ginger root and squeeze by hand over the soup after miso has been added.

– Cut vegetables more finely and use more water if desired.

– Use liquid from cooking other vegetables, i.e., sweet squash, baked root vegetables, water from blanching vegetables, etc. These cooking waters make the soup much sweeter.

Lentil Soup

1 cup green or brown lentils
1 handful wakame, crumbled, or soaked and chopped
1 to 2 medium onions, sliced in crescents
1 carrot, chopped
broccoli stalks or cauliflower stem and core, cut finely
1 stalk celery, chopped
4 to 5 cups water
1 pinch sea salt
1 Tbsp. barley or rice miso
1 handful fresh parsley or scallion, chopped

Wash lentils in a sieve under cold running water. Place wakame in the bottom of the pot, then onions, carrot, broccoli or cauliflower pieces, celery, and lentils in that order. Add water and salt. Bring to a boil, reduce heat to low and simmer, covered, for 40 to 50 minutes.

Puree mixture in a sieve or colander, or leave as is. Dilute miso in a small amount of broth or water and add to mixture. Add more miso, if desired, and more water if soup is too thick. Simmer for 6 to 8 minutes. Serve garnished with parsley or scallions.

Variations and Serving Suggestions:

– Use leftover pureed lentil soup to make a gravy.

– Mix with leftover grains and nuts for a loaf.

– Serve with blanched or steamed broccoli or cauliflower florets, brown rice, and delicatta squash rings or other sweet squash.

Mochi Ball Soup

sesame oil
4 to 5 onions, finely cut in crescents
8 to 10 fresh mushrooms or 5 to 6 dried shiitake mushrooms, soaked in hot water to cover for 10 to 15 minutes
5 cups water
6-inch piece kombu, soaked in water to cover
1 to 1½ Tbsp. shoyu
6 to 8 oz. dried mochi

Heat a small amount of sesame oil in a pot. Add onions and saute 3 to 4 minutes or until onions are translucent. Slice mushrooms and add to onions; saute another 2 minutes.

Add water, kombu, and soaking water. Bring to a boil, cover pot and reduce heat to low. Simmer 30 minutes or until onions are very soft. Remove kombu and save for cooking with beans or vegetables. Season soup with shoyu to taste.

About fifteen minutes before serving soup, cut mochi in 1-inch cubes and place on a cookie sheet. Bake at 450°F for 8 to 10 minutes or until mochi cubes puff up and get slightly crisp.

Place soup in individual bowls and drop 3 mochi squares in each bowl.

Sweet White Onion Miso Soup

10 cups soup stock (water from cooking vegetables)
8 cups white onions, cut in crescents
2 Tbsp. white or yellow miso
scallions or parsley, minced

Bring water and onions to a boil. Simmer, covered, over medium heat for 1 to 1½ hours or until onions are soft and tender.

Remove 1 cup soup liquid. Dissolve miso in liquid, stirring to remove lumps. Add mixture back to soup pot and simmer 3 to 4 minutes. Do not boil. Serve garnished with minced scallions or parsley. Serves 12.

Miso Minestrone

1 to 2 onions, cut finely
2 carrots, chopped finely
½ cauliflower, including core and greens, cut finely
1 handful wakame, crumbled, or soaked and chopped
1 rutabaga, chopped finely
¼ head cabbage
water or stock to cover
1 cup cooked pasta or brown rice (optional)
½ to 1 tsp. red miso per cup of soup
parsley or scallions, chopped finely

Bring vegetables and water to a boil. Simmer, covered, 30 to 40 minutes over low heat. Add pasta or rice and more water if soup is too thick.

Dissolve miso in a bowl of the broth. Add it back to the pot and simmer 5 minutes. Red miso gives it a nice meaty taste. Serve garnished with parsley or scallions.

Miso Soup

[handwritten: All the soups!! use barley miso]

Miso soup is generally eaten daily on a macrobiotic diet. It is thought to help alkalinize the blood, strengthen the body, aid digestion and assimilation, and discharge toxins from the body. Serve the soup as the first course of a meal to prepare the stomach for digestion.

The main ingredient of miso is soybeans which contain up to 34 percent protein — nearly twice as much as meat or fish. Soybeans are also rich in calcium, phosphorus, iron, other minerals, and lecithin. They contain all the amino acids essential to our diet.

There are three main varieties of miso: barley or mugi miso, used throughout the year, made with barley and soybeans; rice or genmai miso, a lighter miso used in warmer, summer weather, made with rice and soybeans; and hatcho miso made with soybeans only, the heaviest and richest of the miso types and used in cold weather.

Miso can be added to any soup. Just before serving, dissolve the miso in a small amount of the soup stock and add to the soup. Start by adding a small amount of miso, adding more if needed but not so much that the soup tastes salty. The miso should mingle with the flavor of the soup and enhance but not overpower it. Simmer the soup for 3 minutes after adding the miso.

Creamy Root Soup

4 large carrots, cut in chunks or wedges
4 large parsnips, cut in chunks or wedges
1 large onion, cut in crescents
1 small handful wakame, crumbled (optional)
4 to 5 cups water
1 to 2 Tbsp. white, yellow, or light barley miso
fresh parsley or scallions, chopped

Place carrots, parsnips, onion, wakame if desired, and water in a pressure cooker and pressure cook 25 minutes. Mash with a large spoon or a potato masher, or press through a sieve or strainer. Add more water if mixture is too thick. Bring to a boil.

Dissolve miso in a small amount of water or soup. Add to vegetables and simmer 4 to 5 minutes; do not boil. Serve in bowls, garnished with chopped parsley or scallions.

Rutabaga Soup

3 to 4 cups stock or water
5-inch piece kombu
2 or 3 onions, chopped
2 or 3 small rutabagas, cubed
1 tsp. barley or rice miso per cup of soup
scallions, minced, or daikon, grated (optional)

Boil soup stock with kombu for 20 to 30 minutes. Cut kombu into fine pieces and return to soup. Add onions. Add rutabagas and simmer, covered, for about 30 minutes or until rutabagas are soft but not soggy.

Remove about ½ cup hot broth. Dissolve miso in broth,

then add back to soup. Simmer about 5 minutes, being careful not to boil soup. Pour soup into individual bowls. Garnish with scallions or daikon.

Rutabaga and Squash Soup

1 handful wakame, crumbled, or soaked and chopped
2 small onions or 1 large onion, cut in crescents
2 large rutabagas, cubed
1 small buttercup squash or ¼ acorn squash, peeled and
   cubed
6 cups water
1½ to 2 Tbsp. barley miso or brown rice miso
fresh parsley, chopped

Add wakame, onions, rutabagas, squash, and water to a pot. Bring to a boil, then reduce heat and simmer, covered, 30 to 40 minutes, or until vegetables are soft.

Remove a bowl of hot soup, dissolve miso in it and add it back to soup. Add more miso if necessary. Simmer 4 to 5 minutes but do not boil. Garnish with parsley.

Serve with rice, beans or tofu, and steamed greens.

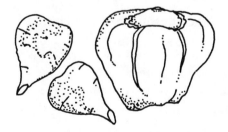

Smooth Squash Soup

5 to 6 cups squash, peeled and cut in chunks (buttercup, Hokkaido pumpkin, or kabocha)
4 to 5 cups water
6-inch piece kombu
1 to 1½ Tbsp. light miso or barley miso
fresh parsley, chopped, or toasted and crumbled nori

Place squash, water, and kombu in a pot. Cover and bring to a boil. Reduce heat to medium-low and simmer until squash is soft and tender, 15 to 30 minutes. Remove kombu and save for cooking with beans.

Puree squash in a food mill, or mash through a colander or sieve with a large wooden spoon. Return puree and liquid to pot and heat to just below boiling point. Dissolve miso in a small amount of puree and add to soup. Simmer for 6 to 8 minutes but do not boil. Place in individual serving bowls and garnish with parsley or nori.

Squash Bisque

3 acorn or delicatta squash, cut in chunks
5 cups water
3 to 4 large onions, cut finely in crescents
2 to 4 cups water or stock
1 to 2 Tbsp. white or yellow miso
minced parsley

Place squash in pot with 5 cups water, bring to a boil, reduce heat, and simmer, covered, 20 to 30 minutes or until soft. Puree in a food mill, or press through a strainer. Return the puree to a pot and add onions and 2 to 4 cups water. Cover and cook over medium heat 20 to 40 minutes. If soup is too thick, add more water.

Dissolve miso in small bowl of warm soup. Add this to the soup and mix well. Simmer 3 to 4 minutes. Do not boil. Pour into soup bowls and garnish with minced parsley. Serves 10 or more.

Squash and Onion Soup

2 Tbsp. light sesame oil or corn oil
7 cups chopped onion
6 cups squash pieces (use delicatta, kabocha, Hokkaido or
    other sweet squash)
8 to 9 cups water or liquid from cooking vegetables
2 to 4 Tbsp. yellow, mellow, or sweet rice miso
1 Tbsp. kuzu
¼ cup cold water

Saute onion in oil 6 to 8 minutes or until golden. Add squash pieces and water; bring to a boil, then simmer, covered, for 1 to 1½ hours.

Puree squash and onions in a blender. Pour back in the pot and bring to a boil. Dissolve kuzu in cold water, add to soup and simmer until thickened.

Dissolve miso in a small amount of soup. Add to pot and simmer 3 to 4 minutes. Do not boil.

Salads

How to Make Blanched or Boiled Salads

Boiled salads are light, tasty salads of assorted blanched greens and other vegetables. They are mineral-rich and very lightly cooked to retain taste, texture, color, and nutrients. The cooking water which may be lightly salted can be saved in jars or used immediately for soup stock.

It is best to cut vegetables in small pieces so they cook quickly and result in a light salad. Use different shapes, such as rounds, matchsticks, cubes, wedges, or other designs. Cook each vegetable separately to retain flavor and color. If you are using very strong tasting or brightly colored vegetables, cook them last so they don't overwhelm or taint the other vegetables. For example, celery and mustard greens have strong flavors, and purple cabbage will turn the water purple, so these vegetables should be cooked last.

Bring the water to a boil and add a few pinches of sea salt, if desired. The water in the pot should be at a high boil when you add the vegetables. Cook each vegetable for 30 seconds to 3 minutes maximum. Most vegetables are done in 1 to 2 minutes. Remove them immediately from the water. Use a basket or large slotted spoon to lift the vegetables out of the water when they are done. The vegetables may be placed on a platter or in a colander to cool.

Use the same water to repeat the process. The more vegetables cooked in the same water, the sweeter and richer the liquid will be for use in soup. Cool vegetables before serving. Layer them on a platter or bowl, attractively arranged to enhance color contrasts. Serve with roasted ground seeds, brown rice vinegar, and/or umeboshi red plum vinegar, or seed dressings.

Suggested Combinations:

– Kale, cabbage, leeks;

– Cauliflower florets and greens, green peas, leeks (cut finely), carrot matchsticks;

– Kale, cauliflower florets, leeks, and carrot pieces;

– Broccoli, cabbage, daikon rounds, minced carrots;

– Purple cabbage, broccoli, daikon or carrot matchsticks;

– Red or purple cabbage, kale, cauliflower, carrot and/or daikon;

– Broccoli, corn cut off the cob, green beans, carrot pieces;

– Kale, corn off the cob, carrot matchsticks;

– Green cabbage, fresh Brussels sprouts cut in thin, round slices, daikon or carrot matchsticks;

– Kale, leeks, cauliflower.

Alfalfa Salad

1 to 2 Tbsp. olive oil
1½ Tbsp. umeboshi vinegar
1½ Tbsp. water
5 cups alfalfa sprouts

Mix oil, vinegar, and water; pour over sprouts and mix with hands.

Blanched Salad

¼ to ⅓ head Chinese cabbage, cut in strips
1 to 1½ summer squash, cut in diagonal pieces
6 to 8 red radishes, quartered
greens from one fresh cauliflower, cut finely
3 stalks celery, chopped
½ to ¾ cup pumpkin seeds, roasted

Shoyu Ginger Dressing:

1½ tsp. juice from freshly grated and squeezed ginger root
1 Tbsp. shoyu
⅓ cup water or to taste

Pour water in a pot to a depth of 5 inches. Bring to boil and cook each vegetable separately: cabbage, 1 minute; squash 2 to 2½ minutes; radish, 1 minute; cauliflower greens, 1 minute; celery, 1 minute. Water must boil continuously with lid off. For best results use large slotted spoon or wire basket to remove vegetables.

Arrange vegetables in layers on serving platter. Do not toss or mix. Sprinkle with dressing.

Broccoli, Pumpkin Seed, and Cabbage Salad

Cut cabbage finely and blanch for 1 to 2 minutes in boiling water, followed by broccoli 2 to 3 minutes (cut into pieces or blanched whole and cut later). Toss with ground, freshly-roasted pumpkin seeds. Add shisho leaf condiment and umeboshi vinegar diluted with an equal amount of water.

Green Bean, Brussels Sprout, and Cauliflower Salad

4 to 5 cups water
4 to 5 cups Brussels sprouts
1 medium cauliflower
2 cups green beans, cut finely in long strips

Bring water to a boil. Meanwhile, peel outer leaves from Brussels sprouts, cut off nubby ends, then slice each sprout lengthwise in thin rounds. Add pieces to the boiling water in two batches, cooking each batch 1 to 2 minutes. Make sure sprouts are submerged. Do not overcook. Remove them with a large slotted spoon and spread them on a plate or platter to cool.

Cut cauliflower florets and leaves in fine pieces. Add them to boiling water and cook 1 to 2 minutes, pressing them down to submerge them. Remove the pieces and place on top of Brussels sprouts.

Boil green beans 2 to 3 minutes or until tender; remove and place them on top of other vegetables.

Serve with a seed dressing or brown rice vinegar with roasted sunflower or pumpkin seeds.

Green, White, and Orange Boiled Salad

4 to 5 cups water
1 bunch kale, cut finely in strips
1 small cauliflower, cut in florets
2 medium leeks, washed well, then cut in thin rounds
3 to 4 carrots, cut in thin rounds

Boil kale pieces 1 minute or until tender; remove. Boil cauliflower florets for 2 to 2½ minutes; remove and place on a plate or bowl to cool. Pour any excess liquid that settles in the bowl back into the pot.

Continuing to keep water boiling, add leeks and boil 1 to 2 minutes; remove. Add carrot pieces, boil 1 minute or until tender, then remove. Save cooking water for soup stock.

Layer vegetables in a bowl or on a serving platter. Place kale on bottom, then add leeks followed by cauliflower and carrot pieces. Serve with Lime Vinaigrette or Seed Dressing.

Tips:

– To clean leeks, cut down the center, about three-fourths of the way through. Rinse well to remove dirt from the inner leaves.

Marinated Vegetable Salad

5 cups broccoli or cauliflower florets (or mixture of both)
carrots, cut in matchsticks or cubed, to make 3 cups
4 celery stalks, minced
3 scallions, cut on diagonal
1½ Tbsp. toasted sesame oil
⅓ cup umeboshi vinegar
¼ cup water
¼ cup lemon juice
½ to 1 tsp. dried oregano
½ to 1 tsp. dried dill weed or basil

Boil water in large pot. Blanch each vegetable separately: broccoli or cauliflower, 2 to 3 minutes; carrots, 1 to 2 minutes; celery, 1½ minutes. Place vegetables in a bowl; add scallions.

Mix remaining ingredients and pour over vegetables. Let sit at least 30 minutes, preferably several hours, before serving.

Potato Asparagus Sauteed Salad

1 cup asparagus, cut in diagonals
1 Tbsp. olive oil
1½ celery stalks, chopped
1 scallion, minced
½ tsp. white, light, or mellow miso
¼ cup water
3 to 4 small potatoes, boiled and crumbled, or cut in pieces
1 Tbsp. toasted sesame seeds

Lightly blanch asparagus for 1 to 2 minutes. Place oil in pan over medium-high heat; add asparagus. Stir 1 to 2 minutes; add celery and scallions and stir 1 to 2 minutes. Dilute miso in water and add with potatoes. Stir, then turn off heat when liquid is absorbed. Sprinkle with sesame seeds. Serves 2.

Radish Top Salad

greens from 3 bunches of radishes, including stems
2 to 3 cups water
1 pinch sea salt
½ cup roasted sesame seeds, ground
1 Tbsp. shoyu
1 Tbsp. water

Boil radish greens in water with salt for 4 minutes, then drain and cut into ½-inch lengths. Mix ground sesame seeds with greens. Combine shoyu and 1 tablespoon of water, and sprinkle mixture over greens. Serve with sweet root vegetables and grains and beans if desired.

Vegetables and Beans

Vegetables

Whole Cooked Brussels Sprouts

Trim off rough end and cut an "X" into the stem end of each sprout. Add water to a skillet to a depth of ¼ inch. Place a 4-inch strip of kombu in the skillet with Brussels sprouts on top. Cover and cook over low heat until sprouts are tender; 10 to 15 minutes.

Burdock and Kombu
A warming winter condiment.

- 5-inch piece kombu
- 2¼ cups water
- 2 Tbsp. shoyu
- 2 long burdock roots, cut in ½-inch lengths and halved lengthwise (2 cups)
- ½ to 1 tsp. mirin (optional)

Soak kombu and cut it into small pieces. Save soaking liquid for cooking. Bring kombu, water, shoyu, and burdock to a boil and cook over low heat 1½ hours. Add mirin during the last few minutes, and cook until most of the liquid is absorbed. If after 1½ hours it is not cooked away, cook with lid off for 15 to 30 minutes more. Store in a jar in the refrigerator, and use a little every day or so as desired.

Serving Suggestions:

– Serve this as a condiment — a few tablespoons with a meal of cooked vegetables and rice or other whole grain with or without beans.

Kinpira

1 tsp. toasted sesame oil or safflower oil
½ tsp. sesame oil (not toasted)
1 Tbsp. sesame seeds
2 Tbsp. soy sauce
2 tsp. mirin (optional)
1 cup carrots, slivered
2 cups burdock, slivered

Combine ingredients in a frying pan. Bring temperature to medium-high. When ingredients start to sizzle, stir for 7 minutes. It is done when vegetables are slightly limp.

Serve as a side dish with brown rice or double recipe and serve as an entree. Serves 3.

Paul Motoyoshi

Cabbage Rolls

Blanch cabbage leaves and cool. Remove hard part of each leaf by cutting out a "V". Place 1 cabbage leaf with "V" cutout closest to you. Place a small, compacted chunk of cooked rice or other filling in center. Fold in edges on outside to cover rice. Roll away from you to make a small oblong or log-shaped roll. Continue filling cabbage leaves.

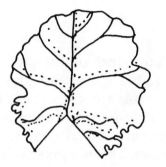

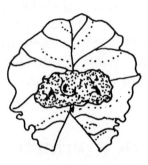

Variations:

– Fill rolls with:

- Warm rice mixed with chopped, roasted walnuts;
- Rice with roasted sunflower seeds;
- Pan-fried rice, celery, onion, sunflower seeds or pumpkin seeds;
- Rice cooked with wheat berries.

– Serve Walnut Miso Gravy over rolls.

Carrot Butter

Cook sliced carrots in a pot with ¼ to ½ inch of water to which a piece of kombu has been added. Cover and cook over low heat 1 to 1½ hours until carrots are soft and can be mashed with a fork. Add umeboshi paste to taste and sesame seeds that have been roasted and ground. Mixture will keep in the refrigerator for 2 or 3 days. This is a good accompaniment with greens.

Carrot Confetti

¼ to ½ tsp. sesame oil
4 cups grated carrot (5 to 6 medium carrots)
½ cup fresh parsley, rinsed and cut finely
½ to ¾ tsp. shoyu
1 to 3 tsp. water, as needed

Turn burner on high. Brush skillet with sesame oil; add carrots and stir gently with chopsticks for 2 minutes. Reduce heat to medium, add parsley and shoyu, and continue stirring gently. Add water to avoid burning vegetables. Stir 3 to 4 minutes more, until vegetables are tender-crisp.

Serving Suggestions:

– Serve warm as a condiment or side dish with cooked beans, rice, or barley and rice, steamed greens, corn bread or corn chips, buttercup, acorn, kabocha, or delicatta squash, and pickles or sauerkraut.

Carrot Matchsticks

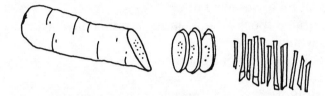

Cut carrot in diagonals of equal thickness. Pile diagonals loosely overlapping each other and cut through them lengthwise in matchstick shapes.

Brush skillet lightly with oil. Heat and add carrot matchsticks. Saute, using chopsticks to stir, for about 5 minutes. Add a small amount of water if necessary. Add a dash of shoyu and ginger juice, then turn off burner. Cover and let sit 1 to 2 minutes before serving.

Serving Suggestions:
– Sprinkle roasted sesame seeds or ao-nori flakes on top at the end of cooking time.

Carrots and Parsley

5 or 6 carrots, cut in matchsticks
sea salt
1 or 2 handfuls parsley, minced

Place carrots in a steamer or in a pot with ¼ inch of water. Sprinkle with 2 pinches of sea salt. Place parsley on top. Steam until tender-crisp (not soggy) about 15 minutes.

Cauliflower "Cheese" Bake

1 head cauliflower
⅓ cup tahini or sesame butter
⅓ cup grated mochi; plain, garlic or millet flavored
⅓ cup water
1 Tbsp. white miso or light miso

Clean cauliflower by removing leaves and stems (save them for boiled salad or sauteed vegetables). Boil cauliflower whole in several inches of lightly salted water or turn upside down and steam 8 to 10 minutes. Place cauliflower in baking dish that has been lightly brushed with oil.

Mix remaining ingredients to make a sauce. Pour sauce over cauliflower. Bake uncovered at 350°F for 30 minutes. Cut and serve from the baking dish. Serve topped with chopped scallions or parsley.

Corn-on-the-Cob

Cook whole ears of sweet corn by steaming 10 to 15 minutes

or until slightly tender. Cut each ear in four pieces; lightly spread small amount of umeboshi paste on each piece. Serve immediately. Leftovers are good the next day.

Dried Daikon and Onion

1 cup dried sliced daikon radish
1½ cups warm water
6-inch piece kombu, soaked and cut finely with knife or
    scissors (optional)
oil (optional)
1½ to 2 large onions, cut in crescents
1½ tsp. shoyu
ginger juice, to taste (optional)

Soak daikon with water and kombu for 30 to 60 minutes. Brush skillet or pot with oil, or pour small amount of soak water into pot. Saute onion pieces until translucent, stirring gently with chopsticks. Add daikon and kombu, and saute 2 to 3 more minutes, then add soak liquid. Turn burner to low heat, cover pot, and cook 30 to 40 minutes. Season with shoyu and ginger juice and simmer 5 to 10 minutes. Remove lid to cook away excess liquid if necessary.

Variation:

– Add more water and more shoyu or miso, plus watercress or scallions to make a delicious onion and dried daikon soup.

Steamed Daikon and Parsley

Cooked daikon is very sweet and tender.

3 cups long white daikon radish, cut in half-moon pieces
1½ cups water
½ to 1 cup minced fresh parsley

Place daikon pieces in a pot. Add water, then place parsley on top. Bring to a boil and cook over medium heat for 5 to 8 minutes or until daikon is tender. Drain off excess water and save for soup.

Serve daikon with rice, beans, and blanched greens or steamed vegetables. Serves 3 to 6.

Daikon Greens with Kale and Sauerkraut

1 to 1½ cups daikon greens (from 3 daikon radishes)
5 kale leaves
water
1 pinch sea salt
2 to 3 Tbsp. natural sauerkraut

Rinse daikon greens and kale and cut finely in strips. Place in a pot with water to a level of ½ to 1 inch. Add salt. Bring to a boil, then reduce heat to medium and cook approximately 5 minutes. Drain off excess liquid, if any, and save it for soup stock.

Top greens with sauerkraut and serve.

Gorgeous Greens

½ to 1 bunch kale or collard greens, cut in ¼-inch strips
2 to 3 leeks, cut in thin diagonals
1 to 2 large daikon or carrots, cut in matchsticks

Dressing:

⅔ cup pumpkin seeds or sunflower seeds, roasted and ground
¾ to 1 Tbsp. umeboshi paste
½ cup or more water
1 Tbsp. rice vinegar

Blanch each vegetable in the order given by immersing in boiling water 1 to 2 minutes. Remove with slotted spoon, drain well and spread in glass serving dish with greens on bottom, leeks in middle, and daikon or carrots on top. Pour dressing over vegetables.

Greens with Miso Mustard

water
½ head cabbage or other greens
1 Tbsp. plus 1 tsp. barley miso
2½ tsp. prepared stoneground natural mustard
2 to 3 Tbsp. warm water
3 Tbsp. sesame seeds, roasted (preferably black sesame seeds)

Bring water to boil in a large pot. Wash and cut cabbage into fine strips. Immerse strips in boiling water to blanch, 1 to 2 minutes. Remove immediately with a slotted spoon or wire basket. Drain cabbage well. Save blanching liquid for soup stock.

Mix miso, mustard, and water; spoon onto greens. Toss well, then sprinkle with sesame seeds.

Rolled Greens

Several different colors of greens can be used, such as dark kale or mustard greens on the outside and white cabbage on the inside. Blanch whole cabbage leaves and other greens in boiling water for 2 minutes, or steam until just lightly done but not soggy. Spread them on a plate to cool. Remove hard part of each leaf by cutting out a "V".

Lay one leaf on sushi mat. Place another one on top to overlap using smaller pieces to fill in. Spread a thin layer of sauerkraut on edge closest to you and roll away from you, squeezing roll with sushi mat. Squeeze completed roll firmly to remove excess liquid. Remove mat and cut roll with a sharp knife into 6 or 8 pieces. Place on plate with cut sides up. Continue making rolls until all leaves have been used.

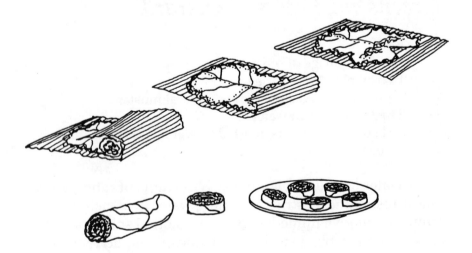

Variation:

– In place of sauerkraut, fill rolls with several heaping tablespoons of roasted, ground sesame seeds to make a rich
side dish.

Boiled Whole Kale Leaves

Boiling kale or other greens in their whole form with a pinch
of sea salt eliminates the bitter taste that often comes from
steaming greens and makes them sweeter.

water to a depth of 1 inch in pot
1 to 3 pinches sea salt
½ to 1 bunch kale (collards, mustard greens, or other greens
can be used)

Place water, salt, and whole greens in pot. Bring to boil at
high heat, then reduce heat to medium or medium high.
Cook with lid on for 3 to 8 minutes (thicker greens take longer). They should be tender but not soggy. Remove greens
from water, saving water for soup stock. Greens will be
sweet.

Variations:

– Sprinkle with brown rice vinegar, or diluted umeboshi
vinegar, and/or ginger juice.

– Top with roasted pumpkin seeds, sesame seeds, or sunflower seeds.

✳ Sauteed Kale and Onion

toasted sesame oil
1 large onion, cut in fine crescents
10 kale leaves, stems removed
3 Tbsp. water
½ to 1 tsp. shoyu

Brush skillet with oil. Saute onion until pieces are translucent.

Wash and cut kale leaves, first in half lengthwise, then lay several leaves on top of each other and cut finely on the diagonal. Add to onions with water. Saute over medium heat 4 to 5 minutes.

Add shoyu and saute 1 to 2 more minutes. Turn off heat and cover skillet until ready to serve.

Serving Suggestions:

– Serve with shoyu-seasoned toasted squash seeds or pumpkin seeds.

– Serve with Lentil Non-Meat Loaf, Pressure-Cooked Brown Rice, and Nishime Sweet Squash.

Kale with Pumpkin Seeds

½ to ⅔ cup pumpkin seeds
dash shoyu or umeboshi vinegar
1 bunch kale

Dry-roast pumpkin seeds in a 300°F oven or in a dry skillet on top of the stove until they pop and turn slightly brown. Sprinkle with shoyu or umeboshi vinegar and stir to coat seeds well. Crush in a suribachi until half of the seeds are broken.

Wash kale and chop into fine pieces. Bring water to a boil and blanch kale 1 to 2 minutes. Top with seasoned roasted pumpkin seeds.

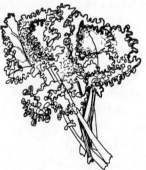

Variations:

– Omit shoyu or umeboshi vinegar and sprinkle brown rice vinegar over steamed kale.

– Leave pumpkin seeds whole.

– Use toasted sesame seeds instead of pumpkin seeds.

– Chop kale into large pieces and steam 5 to 8 minutes.

Steamed Kale and Sauerkraut

1 bunch kale, washed well, cut finely
water
natural sauerkraut

Place one inch of water in a pot. Add kale. Cover and bring to a boil. Boil over medium-high heat 3 to 5 minutes or until kale is tender but not soggy or mushy. Serve mixed with a few spoonfuls of naturally-aged sauerkraut. Allow 1 cup cooked kale per serving.

Kale Stuffed with Sauerkraut

1 bunch kale
natural sauerkraut

Steam whole kale leaves for several minutes, until tender but not soggy; or blanch in rapidly boiling water for 2 minutes. Place ½ to 1 teaspoon sauerkraut on each kale leaf. Fold in the sides of leaves and roll up to make small bundles. They should hold together; if not, insert toothpick through the top.

Kale and Sauerkraut Sandwich

A quick and easy sandwich — good for lunch or a snack.

1 to 2 cups water
1 to 2 cups kale, cut finely
2 slices whole wheat sourdough bread
2 to 3 tsp. tahini or roasted sesame butter
stoneground natural mustard (optional)
2 to 3 tsp. (or to taste) natural sauerkraut

Boil 1 to 2 cups water. Add washed and cut kale. Cover and boil 2 to 5 minutes or until kale is tender. Remove kale from pot and drain well, reserving liquid for soup if desired.

Steam or toast bread, or use it right out of the package or pantry. Spread tahini on both sides of the bread. Spread a thin layer of mustard if desired. Place 1 or 2 leaves of kale on bread. Place a thin layer of sauerkraut on top of kale. Eat it warm or wrap it in plastic and refrigerate.

Variations:

– Steam finely cut cauliflower until soft and add to the kale in the sandwich.

– Spread tahini and mustard in pita bread and stuff with sprouts or kale, cauliflower, and steamed leeks.

– If sauerkraut is too salty, rinse and drain it before placing it in your sandwich.

– Drizzle the steamed kale with brown rice vinegar and omit sauerkraut.

Whole Lotus Seeds

1 cup dry lotus seeds
8-inch piece kombu
4 cups water
1 to 1½ tsp. shoyu

Rinse and soak lotus seeds and kombu in 4 cups of water overnight. Pressure cook 1 hour. Add shoyu and simmer over low heat for 30 minutes. Lotus seeds will be soft but should maintain their shape. Add to grain and vegetable dishes or use as stuffing in Mochi Oven Toast.

Variation:

– Substitute 1 cup dry wakame, soaked 15 minutes, for kombu.

Baked Onions

3 to 4 large onions
2 pinches sea salt
water

Place onions in a baking dish. Add water to a depth of ¼ inch and sprinkle with salt. Cover and bake at 350° to 375°F for 40 to 50 minutes. Check occasionally and add water if needed. Onions are done when knife can be inserted easily. They will be very sweet, almost sugary.

Onion Butter

4 to 6 large onions, cut in crescents
water
2 to 3 pinches sea salt

Place onions in a pot and add water to a depth of ½ inch or to half-cover onions. Bring to a boil, then reduce heat to low and simmer, covered, for 2½ to 8 hours. The longer you cook it, the darker and sweeter it gets. Use lowest heat for longer cooking, and watch so it does not burn. Add a few pinches of salt after about 1 hour. Use as an accompaniment to meals. It will keep for several days in the refrigerator.

Onion Mochi Bake

vegetable oil
1½ squares dried mochi, finely cut
2 medium-large white onions, cut in crescents
1 to 2 Tbsp. water

Brush 9-inch covered baking pan with oil. Add onions; sprinkle mochi on top. Cover and bake at 350°F for 30 minutes. Add a small amount of water to prevent dryness and keep covered 20 to 30 more minutes, until the mochi has melted. Onions will be sweet like candy. Refrigerate leftovers in the summer.

Variations and Serving Suggestions:

– Use turnips in place of onions.

– Use turnips and onions together.

– Bake with sesame seeds on top.

– Sprinkle with gomashio before serving.

– This makes a great breakfast with leftover rice and vegetables.

Onion Pie

Millet Crust (page 70)
5 to 6 large onions, chopped
oil
sea salt or shoyu
kuzu or arrowroot powder (optional)
sesame seeds or walnuts (optional)

Prepare and bake crust. Brush skillet with oil. Saute onions, then reduce heat and cook, covered, with a dash of water for about 45 minutes. Add salt or shoyu to season.

If onion mixture is too watery, add a few spoonfuls of kuzu or arrowroot powder dissolved in water to thicken it. This will make a more sliceable pie.

Spoon mixture into pre-baked crust. Sprinkle sesame seeds or walnuts on top before baking. Bake at 350°F for 15 minutes or until golden brown and sweet smelling.

Baked Parsnips

- 6 parsnips
- sesame oil
- sea salt or shoyu
- roasted sesame seeds or roasted chopped walnuts (optional)

Cut parsnips in long thick strips or moderately thin wedges. Brush each piece with oil and sprinkle with salt or shoyu, if desired. Place on baking sheet and bake at 350° to 375°F for 30 to 40 minutes, until parsnips are very soft and tender. Sprinkle sesame seeds or walnuts on top after baking, if desired.

Tips:

– Leftover Baked Parsnips are good for breakfast, lunch, or snacks.

Baked Squash

- 1 large kabocha, Hokkaido pumpkin, or buttercup squash
- 2 pinches sea salt
- 1 to 1½ cups water

Wash and cut squash in ½-inch pieces, removing seeds. Arrange in a baking dish and sprinkle with salt and water. Cover and bake at 375°F for 45 minutes (or at 400°F for 30 to 35 minutes) until squash is soft.

Nishime Sweet Squash

This squash is very sweet, like pumpkin pie.

- Hokkaido pumpkin, kabocha, delicatta, buttercup or acorn squash
- 4-inch strip kombu
- sea salt or shoyu

Wash squash, cut in half, and remove seeds. Cut large squash in chunks or small squash in quarters or sixths. Pour water in skillet to a depth of ½ inch; add kombu. Place squash in skillet, bring to a boil, then simmer, covered, until soft. Season with a few pinches sea salt at the beginning or shoyu near the end of cooking time.

For a lunchtime treat, eat like a chunk of watermelon.

Delicatta Squash Rings

Allow ¼ to ½ small delicatta squash per person, and make extra as it's great for breakfast or in pack lunches.

- 3 to 4 delicatta squash
- 2 cups water
- 2 pinches sea salt

Cut squash in ½-inch rings. Remove seeds and pulp, but do not peel. Place in pot with water and salt. Bring to a boil, then cook, covered, over medium heat for 20 minutes or until squash is soft.

Tips and Variations:

– Leftover liquid makes great soup stock or a sweet drink.

– Leftover squash can be refrigerated and eaten the next day. The skin is edible and quite good.

– Fill rings with Millet Stuffing (page 123).

– Use the cooked squash for pie filling.

– Mix the cooked squash with onions, noodles, and tofu for a delicious casserole.

Turnip Mochi Melt

A warming, sweet dish with a cheesy, rich taste.

6-inch piece kombu
½ inch water (in pot)
6 turnips, cut in wedges
1 cup dried millet mochi or brown rice mochi, minced or grated finely
1 pinch sea salt
1 tsp. shoyu

Soak kombu in water 15 minutes. Add turnips and mochi and bring to a boil. Reduce heat to low and simmer, covered, 20 to 25 minutes until turnips are soft and mochi melts. Drizzle shoyu on top; cover and cook 5 to 6 more minutes.

Serving Suggestion:

– Serve with rice, green vegetables, and beans.

Jewel Yam-Cakes

Tastes like sweet potato chips but not as thin. Great for breakfast.

≣ 1 large jewel yam per person
corn or light sesame oil

Cut yam into paper-thin slices or to cardboard thickness.

Brush pan with oil. A large cast iron griddle or skillet works best. Brown yam slices over medium-high heat, turning over with a spatula to crisp the other side.

Place on paper towel-lined plate to absorb oil. Serve plain or drizzled with rice syrup, if desired.

Cabbage, Onion, and Parsnip Saute

≣ 1 large white or purple onion, cut in crescents
¼ head purple or green cabbage, cut finely
2 parsnips, cut in thin half-moon shapes
sesame oil
shoyu or sea salt

Lightly brush vegetable pieces with oil. Layer them in pot; first the onions, then cabbage and parsnips. Saute lightly. Turn heat to low and add a small amount of water to moisten. Cover and cook 15 to 20 minutes. Add a dash of shoyu or a pinch of sea salt about 10 minutes before the end of cooking.

Tips:

– You may use more water, then thicken it with kuzu to produce a sweet, syrupy sauce.

– Leftovers kept in cooking liquid are great with soft rice porridge and sprinkled with umeboshi vinegar.

– Chopped roasted walnuts may be added to the freshly-cooked or leftover vegetables.

Baked Parsnips, Onions, and Carrots

1 or 2 onions
2 or 3 carrots
2 parsnips
1 rutabaga
6-inch piece kombu
1 to 1½ cups water
2 to 3 tsp. kuzu
1 tsp. shoyu

Wash, scrub, and trim vegetables. Cut onion in crescents, carrots and parsnips diagonally, and rutabaga in cubes.

Soak kombu in ½ cup water for 15 to 20 minutes, then place kombu in covered baking dish. Add vegetables on top.

Dissolve kuzu in ½ cup water; add shoyu and pour mixture over vegetables. Cover and bake at 375°F for 30 to 45 minutes, until soft but not mushy. Check occasionally and add water if vegetables appear to be drying out.

Serve sprinkled with toasted sesame seeds or gomashio.

Parsnip, Squash, Onion, and Mochi Melt

6-inch piece kombu
½ inch water (in pot)
2 onions, cut in crescents
4 medium parsnips, cut in diagonal wedges
1 medium delicatta squash, cut in chunks
2 pinches sea salt
3 cubes dried mochi, minced or grated finely
1 tsp. shoyu

Place vegetables and water in pot in order listed. Add salt and mochi. Bring to a boil, then simmer, covered, over low or medium heat 20 minutes. Add shoyu and cook 5 to 10 minutes. Add more water if needed.

Potato Vegie Casserole

8 to 12 russet potatoes
sea salt
3 to 4 carrots
1 bunch broccoli
10 to 15 Brussels sprouts
2 onions, chopped
2 to 3 cloves garlic, minced
1 Tbsp. grated ginger
1 Tbsp. safflower oil
⅓ cup grated mochi
⅓ cup water
1 Tbsp. light miso

Boil potatoes in lightly salted water until soft. Chop carrots and broccoli, and cut Brussels sprouts in half. Steam vegetables until soft.

Saute onions, garlic, and ginger with oil in a skillet. Mash potatoes; stir in onions and vegetables. Place in a casserole dish. Mix mochi, water, and miso to make a sauce. Pour over vegetables. Bake at 375°F for 30 minutes.

Julie Hahs

Nishime Root Vegetables

Nishime is a method of cooking that uses a very small amount of water, only enough to prevent burning, and results in sweet, tender vegetables. The technique is to cook the vegetables over low heat for a longer period of time than would normally be required for steaming or boiling. A strip of kombu seaweed is also added to the cooking water, to enhance the flavor.

carrots
daikon
rutabaga
parsnips
water
4-inch piece kombu
sea salt or shoyu
roasted sesame seeds (optional)

Wash and scrub vegetables, then cut in large wedges or chunks, or leave whole. Pour water in skillet to a depth of ¼ inch; add kombu and vegetables. Bring to a boil, then simmer, covered, over low heat until vegetables are soft, 15 to 20 minutes. Cook with lid off during the last 5 to 10 minutes to allow excess liquid to evaporate. Season with a pinch of salt midway through cooking or with a dash of shoyu during the last 10 minutes of cooking. Roll vegetable chunks in sesame seeds if desired.

Root Stew

3, 12-inch pieces kombu
2 to 3 yellow onions
1 to 2 large rutabagas
4 turnips
10, 6-inch carrots
4 parsnips
1 large daikon
4 to 5 cups water
2 to 3 Tbsp. miso

Cut vegetables in irregular wedges. Layer them in a pot in the following order: kombu, onion, rutabagas, turnips, carrots, parsnips, and daikon. Add water. Cover and simmer for 20 to 30 minutes or until done. Add more water during cooking if necessary to prevent burning and so there will be a few tablespoons of broth for each serving. Just before serving, remove 1 cup of broth, combine with miso and add to stew. Simmer for 3 to 5 minutes.

Julie's Root Stew

6-inch piece kombu
1 large onion, cut in thin crescents
3 carrots, cut in diagonal wedges
3 parsnips, cut in diagonal wedges
3 turnips, cut in crescents
½ inch water (in pot)
2 pinches sea salt
1½ tsp. barley miso
½ cup cold water
1 Tbsp. kuzu or arrowroot powder

Layer vegetables in a pot in order listed. Add water and salt. Bring to a boil and simmer over low heat 25 to 35 minutes or until vegetables are soft.

Dissolve miso and kuzu or arrowroot powder in cold water. Add to stew and stir until thickened. Simmer 3 to 4 minutes more, then turn off heat. Let it sit, then serve with rice, beans, and greens.

Julie Hahs

Pizza

Tomato-less Sauce:
- 6-inch piece kombu
- 1 onion
- 2 carrots
- 2 celery stalks
- 3 cloves garlic
- 4 dry shiitake mushrooms or 10 fresh white mushrooms
- 3 fresh beets
- 2 cups water
- pinch sea salt
- 1 bay leaf
- 1 Tbsp. miso or shoyu
- 2 tsp. umeboshi paste
- oregano and/or basil to taste
- ½ cup fresh parsley

Cut vegetables in large chunks; layer them in a pressure cooker in order given and cover with water. Add salt and bay leaf. Pressure cook 15 to 20 minutes, then boil for 30 minutes or cook in a slow cooker all day. Remove the bay leaf and puree vegetables in a food mill or a blender. Add remaining ingredients and simmer 5 minutes. Makes 5⅔ cups.

Serving suggestions:
- This sauce can be used for lasagna, pizza, spaghetti, or enchiladas.

- Freeze extra sauce and use it "in a pinch."

Recipe used with the kind permission of Jan Daniels from her book, *Whole Meals In A Pinch*, now out of print.

Quick Pizza Dough:

- 2¾ cups whole wheat flour
- ½ tsp. sea salt
- 1 Tbsp. baking powder
- ¾ cup water
- 3 to 4 Tbsp. olive oil

Mix ingredients and knead for 5 minutes. Place on a lightly oiled pizza pan dusted with corn meal or corn flour. Makes one 16-inch pizza.

To make pizza:

- Tomato-less Sauce
- 2 pounds tofu
- 3 carrots, grated
- 1 to 2 cups fresh mushrooms, chopped
- 1 large onion, chopped
- 1½ cups plain mochi, grated
- 4 Tbsp. tahini
- 2 to 3 Tbsp. white, yellow, or mellow miso
- 1½ cups water

Spread tomato-less sauce on pizza dough to desired thickness. Crumble tofu on top and add carrots and mushrooms. Lightly saute or boil onion for 2 to 3 minutes, then place on top. Add mochi. Mix tahini, miso, and water. Pour over pizza and bake at 450°F for 20 minutes or until golden and cheesy on top.

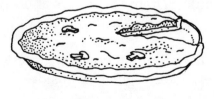

Vegetable Tofu Noodle Bowl

1 Tbsp. toasted sesame oil
1 large onion, minced
12 to 14 oz. tofu
water
2 tsp. white or yellow miso
1 tsp. shoyu
1 to 2 sheets nori seaweed
2 minced green onions or scallions

3 cups red cabbage slices
4 medium carrots, cut into thin rounds
1½ cups green snap peas
1 to 2 tsp. umeboshi vinegar
1 to 2 tsp. water

8 oz. udon noodles, cooked

Heat oil in skillet and saute onions 2 to 3 minutes or until soft. Crumble tofu into onions; add ⅓ cup water a little at a time to moisten, stirring gently to scramble. Add miso and shoyu; cook 2 to 3 more minutes. Crumble nori seaweed into onion-tofu mixture. Continue to stir and cook 1 to 2 minutes. Add minced green onions or scallions; stir, and turn off heat. Cover and set aside.

Layer cabbage, carrots, and peas in a pot. Place ¼ inch of water in pot and bring to a boil. Cover and simmer over medium-high heat 5 to 8 minutes. Drain vegetables and save liquid for soup stock. Toss vegetables with umeboshi vinegar and water.

Arrange udon noodles in individual bowls with scrambled tofu on top of noodles. Place vegetables at side of bowl next to tofu. Serves 2 to 3.

Sea Vegetables

Arame and Almonds

1 cup dry arame
cold water
2 tsp. shoyu or rice vinegar
¼ cup chopped roasted almonds (or walnuts, sunflower
   seeds, or sesame seeds)

Pour water over arame to cover; let it soak 5 to 10 minutes. It
will almost double in size. Place in cast iron or stainless steel
pot with all but the last few tablespoons of soaking water
and bring to a boil, stirring gently with chopsticks or wood-
en spoon. Reduce heat to low and cook, covered, for 20 to 25
minutes. Add shoyu or vinegar and more water if arame is
too dry. If it is too wet, cook, uncovered at higher temperature for 10 minutes or use excess liquid for soup stock.
   Sprinkle nuts or seeds on top and serve.

Variation:

– Cut 3 carrots into matchsticks and add during last 10 to 15
   minutes of cooking. Add shoyu to taste.

Arame with Corn

≣ 1 cup dry arame
2 tsp. umeboshi vinegar
3 ears corn-on-the-cob

Soak arame in cold water to cover for 5 to 10 minutes. Remove and place in a pot with all but the last few tablespoons of soak water, which may be sandy. Simmer, covered, for 15 minutes. Add vinegar and continue to cook 10 minutes or until liquid is absorbed and arame is tender. Remove and place on serving platter.

Boil corn in large pot of water for 4 to 5 minutes or until tender. Cut kernels off the cob, and mix with arame.

Arame and Sauerkraut

≣ 2 cups dry arame
2 cups cold water
1 tsp. shoyu
¼ cup natural sauerkraut

Soak arame 5 to 10 minutes in cold water. Bring to a boil with all but last few tablespoons of soak liquid. Simmer 15 minutes, the add shoyu. Stir, add sauerkraut, and cook 4 to 5 minutes.

Sweet and Sour Arame with Shiitake

This dish is high in calcium, iron, and other minerals.

6 to 7 dry shiitake mushrooms, soaked 20 to 30 minutes in
⅓ cup boiling water
2 cups dry arame, soaked 5 to 10 minutes in 2 cups cold
water
1 Tbsp. mirin (optional)
1 Tbsp. shoyu

Remove stems from mushrooms; discard. Slice mushroom caps finely. Place arame, all but the last few tablespoons of the arame soak water, and mushrooms in a pot. Cover, bring to a boil, then turn heat to medium-low. Simmer 30 minutes.

Add mirin and shoyu. Cook with lid off for 8 to 10 minutes to allow excess liquid to evaporate. Serve as a condiment, allowing 2 to 3 tablespoons per person. Store cooked seaweed in the refrigerator.

Hijiki with Broccoli and Lemon

1 cup dry hijiki
1½ cups cold water
10 to 12 mushrooms, cut in small, thin rounds
2 to 3 tsp. toasted sesame oil
1 Tbsp. shoyu
3 to 4 cups broccoli florets and stalks, chopped
juice of ½ lemon

Soak hijiki in water for 20 to 30 minutes. Saute mushrooms in oil for 2 minutes. Cut hijiki in pieces and add to mushrooms with all but last few tablespoons soaking liquid. Bring mixture to a boil and simmer over low or medium heat, covered, for 30 minutes. Add more water if hijiki starts to dry out. Add shoyu.

Add broccoli pieces and turn heat to medium-high. Cook, covered, 3 to 5 minutes, until broccoli is tender and all liquid has cooked away. Add lemon juice and remove to serving dish. Serves 6 as a side dish.

Serving Suggestions:

– Serve with noodles or rice, cooked carrots and/or corn-on-the-cob, and other vegetables or tofu. If using udon noodles, allow 1 pound of noodles per 5 to 6 people. Toss noodles with a small amount of olive oil or corn oil, if desired.

– Add tofu cubes to mushrooms and hijiki and simmer to make a nice cheesy texture and taste.

Hijiki and Leeks with Pumpkin Seeds

1 cup cold water
1 cup hijiki
1 or 2 large leeks
sesame oil, toasted
1 Tbsp. shoyu, umeboshi vinegar, or sauerkraut juice
½ cup whole pumpkin seeds, roasted

Soak hijiki in cold water 20 to 30 minutes.

Cut leeks down the center about three-fourths of the way through, then rinse under cold running water, pulling leaves apart and rubbing with your finger to remove dirt. Cut in thin diagonal slices and saute in a skillet that has been lightly brushed with oil, stirring gently with chopsticks 2 to 3 minutes.

Drain hijiki, saving liquid. Add hijiki to leeks and saute another 2 to 3 minutes. Add all but the last few tablespoons of soak liquid and shoyu, then cover and simmer over low heat for 35 to 40 minutes. Sprinkle with pumpkin seeds.

Serving Suggestions:

– This dish goes well with:
- brown rice cooked with azuki beans, chickpeas, or black soybeans;
- steamed or blanched cauliflower and cabbage;
- baked squash with chestnut puree.

Helen's Hijiki Salad

½ to 1 cup hijiki
1 onion, diced
1 Tbsp. sesame oil or water
1 medium carrot, diced
2 Tbsp. shoyu
½ cup water
1 parsnip, diced
lemon juice, to taste
4 tsp. chopped scallions or parsley

Wash hijiki and soak 15 minutes. Meanwhile, saute onion in oil or water. Chop hijiki and add to onions with carrots, shoyu, and water to cover. Bring to a boil, add parsnip, and cook over medium-high heat 25 to 30 minutes. Water should be absorbed. Remove from heat and add lemon juice to taste, Garnish with scallions and/or parsley.

Helen Crofton

Beans

Pressure Cooking:

Pressure cooking beans saves time and makes the beans more digestible. Soak chickpeas, azuki beans, or pinto beans overnight in two to three times as much water as beans. Drain and replace soaking water with fresh water. Pressure cook beans with a 6-inch piece of kombu over low heat for 50 to 60 minutes. After beans are tender, season with sea salt, miso, or shoyu and simmer 10 to 20 minutes. Do not pressure cook lentils or split peas; they may block the valve of the pressure cooker.

Boiling:

Soak beans in water overnight, then drain well. Place in a pot with a 6-inch piece of kombu and fresh water to a level of about ½ inch above the beans. Bring beans and water to a boil, shock with ¼ cup cold water to stop the rapid boil, bring to a boil again and repeat shock treatment two or more times. Cover and simmer over low heat for 2 to 3 hours, depending on the type of bean. Check periodically to see if more water is needed. When beans are tender, season with sea salt, miso, or shoyu and simmer 10 to 20 minutes.

Black beans, azuki beans, pinto beans, and navy beans require 1½ to 2 hours of boiling. Chickpeas will need to cook 2 to 3 hours. Black soybeans need 2 to 3½ hours of boiling to be soft and digestible. Lentils and split peas need no presoaking. They take 1 to 1½ hours to cook.

Tips:

– Remember to cook the beans with a piece of kombu seaweed to help prevent gas and cut down on cooking time.
  The kombu will dissolve or at least break up so that it is almost unnoticeable.

– Do not stir beans during cooking or they will become
  mushy and lose their shape.

– After beans are tender and seasoning has been added, you
  may place cut carrots, onions, sweet squash, or other vegetables on top of beans and simmer 20 to 30 minutes until
  vegetables are tender.

– Azuki beans are especially delicious seasoned with shoyu.

– Pinto beans are enhanced with a sweet flavor by adding
  white, yellow, mellow, or natto miso.

Baked Anasazi Beans

A native American bean that has been re-popularized.

6 cups anasazi beans, soaked overnight and drained
10 cups water
6-inch piece kombu
¼ cup ginger juice
¼ to ½ cup barley miso, or to taste
¼ to ⅓ cup barley malt, or to taste

Using at least a 6-quart pressure cooker, or cooking in two
batches, pressure cook beans in fresh water with kombu for
45 to 50 minutes. Place in large oven dishes or baking pans.

Mix ginger juice, miso, and barley malt syrup, adding 3
tablespoons of syrup and tasting to see if more is desired.
Stir into beans with cooking liquid and bake at 325°F for 1

hour or at 200°F for several hours. Garnish with chopped scallions before serving if desired. Serves 12 to 14.

Serving suggestions:
– Serve with rice and/or corn bread or tortillas.

– Use baked beans to make tacos or enchiladas.

Baked Azuki and Black Beans

2 cups cooked azuki beans
4 cups cooked black beans
2 to 3 Tbsp. ginger juice, squeezed from grated fresh ginger
3 Tbsp. red miso
1½ to 2 cups water
2 Tbsp. barley malt syrup or powder

Mix cooked beans, ginger juice, miso dissolved in a small amount of warm bean liquid, water, and barley malt syrup. Place in ovenproof casserole dish or 9" x 14" x 1" pan. Cover and bake at 250°F for several hours or until liquid is absorbed and beans are soft and chewy, or bake at 350° to 375°F for 1 hour. Stir several times during baking to prevent burning or hardness on top.

Azuki Burgers

Mix cooked azuki beans with any of the following combinations:

– Cooked millet, finely chopped carrot and onion;

– Cooked rice, finely chopped celery, grated carrot, flaxseed, shoyu, ginger juice;

– Cooked buckwheat groats, flaxseed, chopped parsley, chopped carrot, sunflower seeds (optional), ginger juice, shoyu, dash of oil.

Add flour if mixture is too wet; water if mixture is too dry. Form into patties. Pan-fry both sides in a lightly oiled skillet over medium-high heat until golden brown, or broil or bake in oven.

Azuki Quiche

Millet Crust:

2 cups soft cooked millet
⅓ cup sunflower seeds, ground
2 to 3 pinches sea salt
hot water

Preheat oven to 350°F. Mix ingredients, adding water to make a doughy consistency. Mix with spoon or your hands to blend well. Spread in a lightly oiled pie pan, then bake 15 to 30 minutes. Sprinkle a few drops of water on crust if it appears to be too dry.

Filling:

Mix cooked azuki beans with one or more of the following:
- onions
- carrots
- squash
- chestnuts
- apples and raisins
- mushrooms and onions

Or use leftover azuki, kombu, squash mixture.

Mash beans and other ingredients with a potato masher or in a hand-operated food mill. Spoon mixture into prepared crust and bake 15 to 20 minutes at 350°F.

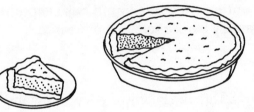

Serving Suggestions:

– Serve as an entree accompanied by brown rice and steamed greens or broccoli, plain or sprinkled with rice vinegar or diluted umeboshi vinegar.

Mexican Beans

1 cup azuki beans
1 cup black turtle beans or black soybeans
6-inch piece kombu
4 cups or more water
2 to 3 Tbsp. barley miso
chopped scallions or parsley (optional)

Rinse and soak beans overnight; drain. Place kombu in pressure cooker. Add beans and fresh water to a level of 1 inch above beans. Pressure cook 1 hour, then turn off burner.

Stir miso into beans. Bake in an open casserole dish at 325° to 350°F until most of the liquid has evaporated. Mix in scallions or parsley before serving, if desired.

Tips:

– You can refrigerate the beans after cooking and bake the next day.

– Combine equal parts black beans, pintos, and azukis.

Black Bean Tacos

Black Bean Filling
Taco Vegies
Tofu Guacamole (page 171)
brown rice, cooked
corn tortillas

Black Bean Filling:

- ½ to 1 Tbsp. light sesame oil
- 1 to 2 medium onions, cut finely
- 5 to 6 cups cooked black beans; or use Baked Azuki and
  Black Beans (page 69) or Anasazi Beans (page 68)
- water
- shoyu

Lightly oil pan; add onions and saute until soft. Add beans and stir. Add water if necessary; add shoyu to taste and stir. Cook away excess liquid.

Taco Vegies:

- ½ to ⅔ head cabbage, cut finely
- 4 carrots, cut in matchsticks
- 5 or 6 stalks broccoli, chopped
- umeboshi or rice vinegar
- alfalfa sprouts

Boil water; blanch cabbage 1 to 2 minutes; remove and place in serving bowl. Blanch carrots, then blanch broccoli and place in a separate bowl. Sprinkle vinegar over carrots and broccoli. Reserve alfalfa sprouts for garnish.

Assembling Tacos:

Warm corn tortillas in oven. Place rice in tortillas, then several tablespoons beans, a spoonful of Tofu Guacamole; and blanched cabbage or sprouts. Serve with broccoli and carrots on the side. Serves 8 to 10 people.

Black Bean Enchilada Pie

8 to 10 yellow corn tortillas
4 to 5 cups black beans, cooked
2 cups carrots, cooked
dash shoyu
1 onion, lightly sauteed
$\frac{1}{4}$ to $\frac{1}{2}$ lb. tofu, crumbled (optional)
$\frac{3}{4}$ cup grated mochi
2 Tbsp. tahini
1 Tbsp. white or yellow miso
$\frac{3}{4}$ cup water

Lightly oil a 9-inch pie pan or square baking pan. Arrange 4 or 5 tortillas on the bottom.

Puree beans and carrots together. Add onion, and place mixture on top of tortillas. Place another layer of tortillas, followed by another layer of beans. Add crumbled tofu and grated mochi. Combine tahini, miso, and water and pour over the top.

Cover and bake 20 minutes at 325° to 350°F, then uncover and bake 10 to 15 minutes.

Tips:

– This pie can be assembled ahead of time, chilled several hours or overnight, then baked just before serving.

– Leftovers are good cold in a pack lunch, for breakfast, or for a quick meal.

Chickpea Roll-ups

1½ cups chickpeas, soaked overnight and drained
3 to 4 cups water
2 tsp. sesame oil or toasted sesame oil
1 large onion, cut finely
1½ to 2 Tbsp. white or yellow miso or 1 Tbsp. barley miso
scallions or green onions, minced
1 bunch kale or mustard greens, cut finely
8 to 12 whole wheat tortillas or chapatis

Cook chickpeas in water until tender, or pressure cook 1 hour. Drain and reserve ⅔ to 1 cup cooking liquid.

Heat oil in a skillet; add onions and saute until translucent. Add chickpeas and reserved liquid and stir well. Cook 5 to 6 minutes. Add miso and simmer 3 to 4 minutes. Turn off heat and garnish with scallions.

Steam kale or mustard greens or lightly saute in a skillet brushed with oil. Add a few drops of shoyu if desired.

Place several heaping spoonfuls of chickpea and onion mixture on each tortilla or chapati. Top with a few tablespoons kale or mustard greens, and roll up. Fasten each roll-up with two toothpicks. Repeat until all ingredients are used.

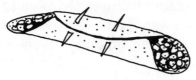

Serving Tip:

– Serve two roll-ups per person with a light salad for a quick and summery meal.

Chickpeas and Squash

3 cups chickpeas, soaked overnight and drained
6-inch piece kombu
3 cups water
½ large squash (6 to 7 cups), cubed (use buttercup or
    kabocha squash, or Hokkaido pumpkin)
1 Tbsp. shoyu or 1½ Tbsp. miso

Place chickpeas, kombu, and fresh water in a pressure cooker. Pressure cook for 1 hour or until beans are tender. Add squash and simmer, covered, for 15 to 20 minutes. Add shoyu or miso dissolved in a small amount of water. Simmer 5 to 10 minutes, and remove lid if too much liquid is present.

Serve with greens, rice or millet or barley, or a combination of any two grains.

Tips and Variations:

– Leftover mixture becomes even sweeter. It can be served at room temperature.

– Use onions or a mixture of onions, carrots, and/or turnips in place of squash.

– Add kuzu for a creamy texture: Dissolve 1 tablespoon kuzu in ½ cup cold water; add to pot when vegetables are soft and when you are adding miso or shoyu. Stir and cook until thickened.

– Make a creamy soup: Puree, adding water and more miso to season soup. Leftover soup keeps for a week in the refrigerator. Garnish with fresh parsley when serving.

– Puree or mash to make a pie filling.

Baked Cheesy Chickpeas

3 cups cooked chickpeas, drained
1½ cups liquid from chickpeas or liquid plus water
2 to 3 Tbsp. tahini or sesame butter
2 Tbsp. white miso
5 oz. plain mochi, grated or finely minced

Place chickpeas in a casserole dish. Make sauce from tahini, miso, mochi, and chickpea liquid. Pour over chickpeas. Bake at 325°F for 20 minutes.

Serving Suggestions:

– Serve with brown rice or rice with wheat berries, or udon noodles, steamed carrots with parsley, steamed broccoli or kale and natural sauerkraut or daikon pickle.

Quick-n-Easy Lentil Loaf

Makes 2 loaves — good for quick meals or to have lunch fixings on hand.

2 to 3 cups cooked lentils
1 cup cooked millet
⅔ to 1 cup cooked hijiki
1 to 2 Tbsp. barley miso
2 to 4 stalks celery, cut finely
2 Tbsp. flaxseed, ground
6 Tbsp. boiling water
sunflower seeds, ground

Mix lentils, millet and hijiki. Add miso and celery.

In a separate bowl pour boiling water over flaxseed and let sit 15 minutes. Whisk or whip it, then add to lentil mixture. It will help bind loaf together. Add sunflower seeds. Place mixture in lightly oiled loaf pans. Bake at 350°F for 30 minutes.

Serving Suggestion:

– Slice and serve with greens, corn-on-the-cob, and soft squash or carrots.

Lentil Non-Meat Loaf

1 cup lentils
1½ cups water
4- to 6-inch piece kombu
2 cups cooked millet
1 cup barley flakes or oat flakes
3 Tbsp. barley miso
3 Tbsp. flaxseed, ground
½ to ¾ cup sunflower seeds, ground
1 to 2 Tbsp. lemon juice
½ to 1 cup fresh parsley, chopped
¾ tsp. oregano
½ to ¾ tsp. dill weed
2 to 3 cloves garlic, minced or pressed

Rinse lentils and add to a pot with water and kombu. Bring to a boil, then simmer, covered, 30 to 40 minutes. Mixture should be soupy; if not, add ¼ cup or more water.

Add cooked millet, barley or oat flakes, miso, flaxseed, sunflower seeds, and lemon juice. Mixture should be very moist.

Mix in parsley and other seasonings (optional). Bake in a covered loaf pan at 350°F for 40 to 45 minutes. Remove cover and bake 10 to 15 minutes more. Cool for 30 minutes. Slice and serve.

Serving Suggestions:

– Serve with whole steamed soft carrots (with diluted umeboshi vinegar, if desired), steamed broccoli, sauerkraut, and brown rice.

Lentil Pate

    1 cup lentils
    3 cups water
    6-inch piece kombu
    miso
    garlic
    greens

Cook lentils with kombu and water for 1 hour, covered, or until lentils are very soft. Check occasionally and add more water if needed.

Add 1 teaspoon miso per 2 cups cooked lentils and mash. Add grated or minced garlic. Mix in chopped spring greens and serve on rice cakes.

Variations:

– Add prepared mustard, sauteed onions, umeboshi paste (diluted), sunflower seeds or ground sesame seeds or roasted and chopped walnuts, and soft cooked carrot.

– Saute 1 large minced onion and 4 to 5 minced garlic cloves; add 4 cups cooked lentils and ½ teaspoon salt. Cover and cook over low heat for 10 to 15 minutes. Add 2 tablespoons tahini and chopped fresh parsley or scallions.

Lentil Curry

6-inch piece kombu
1 cup lentils, rinsed and drained
3 cups water
2 to 3 tsp. olive oil
1 large onion, chopped
1 green pepper, seeds removed, cut finely
1 Tbsp. light miso
$\frac{1}{2}$ tsp. cumin
$\frac{1}{2}$ to 1 tsp. curry powder
$\frac{1}{4}$ tsp. coriander
$\frac{1}{2}$ to 1 cup walnuts, roasted (optional)
chopped scallions or parsley

Bring kombu, lentils, and water to a boil, and cook over medium to low heat for 40 minutes.

Meanwhile, heat skillet with oil. Saute onion until translucent, then add green pepper. Add to lentil pot after lentils have cooked 20 minutes.

When lentils are done, add miso, cumin, curry powder, and coriander. Garnish with walnuts, if desired, and chopped scallions or parsley. Serves 4 to 5.

Serving Suggestions:

– Serve over a bed of brown rice and steamed cauliflower.

– Serve with sweet baked squash or parsnip.

Split Pea Cashew Pate

1½ cups green split peas
½ cup cashews
6-inch piece kombu
3½ cups water
2 to 2½ Tbsp. miso
1 large handful parsley, chopped
2 to 3 cloves garlic, minced (optional)

Place peas, nuts, kombu, and water in a pot. Cover and bring to a boil, then simmer for 1 hour or until peas are very soft.

Mash pea mixture with a large spoon or fork. Add miso, parsley and garlic. Mixture will be very smooth and creamy except for pieces of cashews which add texture, crunch, and flavor. Chill before serving.

Variations and Serving Suggestions:

– Replace split peas and cashews with:
- brown lentils and walnuts;
- azuki beans and almonds;
- yellow split peas and sesame seeds.

– Serve with:
- steamed cauliflower and diagonally sliced carrot rounds;
- finely cut leeks, blanched;
- alfalfa sprouts;
- cucumber rounds;
- wheat or rye crisp bread or pita bread wedges;
- bed of lettuce or other greens.

– Leftover pate can be made into a delicious soup by adding cooked hijiki and liquid.

Pinto Bean Salad

This is a great way to use leftover rice and leftover beans.

1 cup diced celery
1 cup minced onion
1 cup diced carrot
6 cups cooked short-grain brown rice
1 cup cooked pinto beans
1 Tbsp. olive oil or corn oil
1 Tbsp. brown rice vinegar
1 to 2 Tbsp. shoyu
½ cup roasted sunflower seeds or pumpkin seeds (optional)
2 tsp. minced or pressed garlic (optional)

Cook each type of vegetable separately by blanching in boiling water 1 to 3 minutes and removing with a large slotted spoon to drain.

Mix rice, beans, cooked vegetables, oil, vinegar, shoyu, seeds, and garlic. Serve immediately or chill until ready to serve. It will keep several days if refrigerated. Serves 6 to 8.

Pinto Bean Burgers

2 medium onions, chopped
2 Tbsp. oil
2 cups cooked pinto beans
1 Tbsp. shoyu
1 tsp. cumin
½ tsp. dry mustard (optional)
4 Tbsp. chopped parsley
1 cup cooked millet
½ cup wheat germ or sunflower seeds, ground

Saute onions in oil until soft. Mash beans with onions, then add remaining ingredients. Taste for seasoning; adjust as necessary. Shape into six patties and place on baking pan or cookie sheet. Chill 1 to 2 hours or overnight. Grill outdoors or bake in oven on lightly oiled pan at 350°F for 25 minutes or until browned and cooked through.

Variations and Serving Suggestions:

– Use chickpeas instead of pinto beans.

– Substitute 1 teaspoon coriander for mustard.

– Use azuki beans in place of other beans, and add ½ cup chopped celery, omit cumin and/or mustard, or use 1 teaspoon tekka or coriander in place of other spices.

– Serve with:
  - Steamed kale, cabbage, mustard greens, or other fresh greens, with a dash of brown rice vinegar.
  - Carrot soup.

Baked Pinto Beans

2 cups dry pinto beans, soaked overnight and drained
5-inch piece kombu
3 cups water
1½ Tbsp. barley miso
2 Tbsp. powdered or 3 Tbsp. liquid barley malt

Pressure cook beans with kombu and fresh water for 50 minutes, then turn off heat. Drain off ½ to 1 cup excess liquid and reserve.

Place beans in a casserole dish with miso and barley malt. Cover and bake at 200° to 250°F for 1 to 3 hours. Check often; add reserved liquid if beans dry out during cooking.

Serve with rice, chips, and plenty of fresh, lightly cooked vegetables.

Tempeh

Tempeh is a fermented soybean cake which contains the whole bean, fiber, vitamin B_{12}, iron, calcium, and high-quality protein. Tempeh is cholesterol-free and contains only 13 grams unsaturated fat and 7 grams carbohydrate per 4-ounce serving. A serving of tempeh has as much protein as a similar portion of beef or chicken.

Tempeh needs to be cooked with shoyu or in lightly salted water to aid digestion and help with assimilation. A piece of kombu seaweed may be added during cooking and removed before serving. Tempeh is found in the freezer or refrigerator section of natural food stores.

Poached Tempeh

5 cups water
½ to 1 tsp. sea salt or shoyu
6-inch piece kombu
8 oz. tempeh

Heat water; add salt or shoyu and kombu. Add tempeh and cook 30 minutes.

Use immediately or store in refrigerator for a quick meal. Save extra liquid to add to soups.

Tips:

– Steam poached tempeh with vegetables.

– Add poached tempeh to noodles with sauce or to vegetable salads.

– Pan-fry poached tempeh in skillet brushed with oil; add a dash of shoyu and freshly squeezed ginger juice just before serving.

– Cut poached tempeh in ¾-inch cubes. Thread on skewers with cooked cauliflower and broccoli florets, cooked carrot wedges, and whole cooked mushrooms if desired. Spoon Sunflower Thyme Sauce on top.

Tempeh with Mushrooms and Miso Sauce

8 oz. Poached Tempeh (page 86)
2 to 3 tsp. sesame oil or toasted sesame oil
¼ lb. (approximately 4 cups) fresh mushrooms, cut finely
2½ Tbsp. barley miso
2 cups cold water
1 Tbsp. kuzu
¾ cup chopped fresh parsley or minced green onion

Cut tempeh in strips ½ inch wide and ¼ inch thick. Heat oil in large skillet. Add mushrooms and saute 5 to 6 minutes or until soft. Add ¼ to ½ cup water, a little at a time, to keep mushrooms from drying out. Add tempeh, saute 2 to 3 minutes, and add another ¼ to ½ cup water while cooking to keep tempeh and mushrooms moist.

Dissolve miso in 2 cups cold water, then add kuzu and dissolve kuzu. Add this mixture to tempeh and mushrooms; cook, stirring, until thickened. Add parsley or green onion, turn off heat, and cover to let garnish soften.

Serving suggestions:

– Serve over cooked rice, rice and barley, noodles, millet, or
  millet pressed into a loaf pan and sliced.

TLT

Like a BLT with no bacon — actually a Tempeh, Lettuce, and
Tomato. Or try a Tempeh, Kale, and Sauerkraut sandwich.

3 to 4 oz. pan-fried tempeh per person or sandwich
    (Pan-fried Tempeh, page 87)
2 slices whole wheat sourdough or rice bread per sandwich
soy mayonnaise (optional)
stoneground mustard
natural sauerkraut (optional)
lettuce or steamed kale
tomato slices (optional)

Prepare tempeh. Spread each slice of bread with mayonnaise, if desired, followed by a thin layer of mustard. Spread
a dash of sauerkraut on one slice of bread, if desired. Place a
layer of lettuce or steamed kale on bread and top with a
layer of tempeh. Top with more lettuce or kale and a slice or
two of tomato. Put second slice of bread on top.

Tempeh with Onions and Sauerkraut

8 oz. Poached Tempeh (page 86)
1 large onion, cut in crescents
1 to 2 tsp. sesame oil
½ tsp. shoyu
3 to 4 Tbsp. natural sauerkraut

Mince tempeh finely. Saute onion in sesame oil for several minutes, until onions are almost translucent. Add tempeh and saute 1 to 2 minutes, adding a dash of water if needed to prevent burning. Add shoyu, stir, then saute 2 to 3 minutes. Add sauerkraut, stir, and add more water if necessary. Cover and cook over low heat 3 to 4 minutes to allow flavors to mingle.

Serving Suggestions:

– Serve on unyeasted whole grain bread with stoneground mustard and chopped scallions or mustard greens or cooked kale.

– Serve with udon noodles (plain or lightly coated with sesame butter) and steamed broccoli and steamed carrot and parsley on the side.

– Serve rolled up in nori seaweed, sushi style.

– Serve with brown rice, steamed greens, and delicatta squash rings.

Terrific Tempeh Stew

4-inch piece kombu
²/₃ cup water
¹/₃ cup shoyu
8-oz. tempeh
1 large onion, cut in crescents
1 daikon or medium turnip, cut in wedges
1 carrot, cut in irregular wedges
1 rutabaga, cut in wedges
2 pinches sea salt
1 to 1½ Tbsp. kuzu
1 tsp. rice syrup
1 tsp. rice vinegar
1 tsp. or less shoyu
1 tsp. ginger juice (optional)

Rinse kombu and place in bottom of pot with tempeh. Add ²/₃ cup water and ¹/₃ cup shoyu. Bring to a boil and simmer 20 to 30 minutes.

Layer another pot with onions, daikon or turnip, carrot, and rutabaga, in that order. Cut tempeh into cubes and place on top of vegetables. Add some of the tempeh cooking liquid to the pot, and save about ¹/₃ cup for adding later. Sprinkle salt on top, cover, and cook 20 to 30 minutes or until vegetables are somewhat soft.

Dilute kuzu in reserved cooking liquid. Add syrup, vinegar, and more shoyu if desired to make a sweet and sour sauce. Add ginger juice if desired. Add to vegetables and tempeh pot; stir and cook until thickened.

Variations and Serving suggestions:

– Layer onion, carrot, and daikon pieces, and Brussels sprouts, halved.

– Use umeboshi vinegar and shoyu for the sweet and sour sauce.

– Use mirin and shoyu for the sauce.

– Serve with pressure-cooked brown rice tossed with roasted chopped walnuts, sesame seeds or sunflower seeds, and fresh greens on the side.

Tempeh "Cheese" Bake

4 oz. dried mochi
1½ Tbsp. white or yellow miso
1½ cups hot water
2 to 3 Tbsp. tahini or sesame butter
scallions or green onions, minced finely
16 oz. tempeh (soy or 5-grain type)

Grate mochi or mince finely. Dilute white miso in water, then add tahini or sesame butter. Add mochi and scallions; stir.

Cut tempeh in 2" x 1" x ½" strips. Place side by side in a 9" x 13" baking pan. Pour sauce over tempeh. Bake at 350° to 375°F for 30 minutes or until golden. Serves 7 to 8.

Serving Suggestions:

– Serve with brown rice, or rice and wheat berries, or udon noodles, steamed or blanched kale mixed with sauerkraut, and long-cooked chunks of carrot or squash.

✳ *Marinated Tempeh Fingers*

≡   8-oz. tempeh

marinade:
≣   ¾ cup water
      ¼ cup shoyu
      1 to 2 tsp. juice from grated fresh ginger root

or:
≣   ¾ cup water
      3 Tbsp. shoyu
      3 Tbsp. rice vinegar

Cut tempeh in finger-sized pieces. Add one of the marinades: water, shoyu and ginger juice or water, shoyu, and vinegar. Marinate 30 minutes to 1 hour. Turn tempeh pieces over during marination.

Bake, broil, or poach tempeh in the marinade for 15 to 25 minutes. Turn pieces over for uniform cooking.

Variations:

– Roll marinated tempeh in bread crumbs or flour and pan-fry until golden.

– Serve with grated daikon sprinkled with shoyu.

– Serve with prepared mustard or miso mustard on the side with chopped scallion garnish.

– Dip in sauce made of 3 to 4 tablespoons soy mayonnaise, 1 to 2 tablespoons stoneground mustard, and 1 to 2 teaspoons shoyu.

Tofu

Tofu is a high-protein, low-calorie, no-cholesterol product made from the coagulated solids of soybean milk. It is white and soft like some cheeses. It is sold as firm "nigari" tofu, which is excellent for slicing, marinating, and baking; and soft tofu, which is good in quiches, casseroles, sauces, and dips.

Tofu can be a helpful item in making the transition to a vegetarian, non-dairy diet. It contains calcium, phosphorus, B vitamins and even a small amount of fiber. A 4-ounce serving of tofu contains a mere 100 calories, while 4 ounces of cheese contain about 400 calories, 70 to 80 percent of which come from fat.

Soybeans are high in fat when compared with beans like azuki, lentils, and chickpeas, so tofu should be used moderately. Tofu is a refined, processed bean product and is not a whole food; some of the fiber and wholesomeness is lost. Therefore, tofu is best used as an occasional food rather than as a daily staple.

Lest I discourage you from eating tofu instead of whole soybeans, I should point out that soybeans are difficult to digest in their whole form while tofu is much more easily digested and easily prepared.

Tofu is soft, watery, fatty, and has an overall cooling effect on the body. To modify these yin qualities, we can marinate tofu in miso or shoyu and water and bake it, broil it, or pan-fry it. Even if you are using tofu in a sauce or as a dressing, it is best to cook it first, by boiling or steaming.

Tofu can be used in an endless variety of ways. It has the amazing ability to absorb the flavor of whatever it is cooked with, or to which it is added. You can steam it, boil it and press it to remove excess liquid, or saute it in water or a small amount of oil. Use it in quiches, casseroles, lasagnas, and scrambles or pasta sauces in place of eggs, cheese, and sour cream. Try it in stroganoff, with crackers, on pizza or in any other recipe or dish you fancy. It's a chameleon!

Marinated Tofu

1 part rice vinegar
1 part shoyu
2 to 3 parts water
cubed or sliced medium-firm tofu
scallions or water-sauteed parsley, finely cut

Mix liquid ingredients; marinate tofu for 1 hour or longer turning the tofu so all sides are coated with marinade. Bake tofu in the marinade at 350°F for 15 minutes or until tender or crisp as desired. Or broil tofu until light brown. Turn it over in the marinade as it bakes or broils. Or poach tofu in a pan with marinade. Serve with a generous garnish of scallions or parsley.

Variations:

– Add fresh ginger juice to marinade.

– Lightly bread marinated tofu in wheat, corn, rice, or other flour or bread crumbs and pan-fry, or brush with oil and bake.

– Use 1 part ume vinegar and 4 parts water for marinade.

Marinated Tofu Cutlets

  1 to 1½ lbs. tofu
  ½ cup shoyu
  ¼ cup rice vinegar
  1¼ cup water
  1 cup plus 1 Tbsp. arrowroot powder
  pinch sea salt
  2 to 3 Tbsp. rice flour
  water
  mirin (optional)
  sesame oil

Cut tofu in ½-inch slices. Marinate tofu in shoyu, rice vinegar, and water for 30 minutes or longer.

Mix arrowroot powder, sea salt, rice flour, and water to make a paste-like but dippable batter. Add a few dashes of mirin, if desired.

Lightly brush skillet with sesame oil. Dip tofu slices in batter, then pan-fry until tofu is lightly browned.

Baked Garlic Tofu Cutlets

  2½ lbs. tofu cut in ¼-inch slices
  3 cups water
  ½ cup shoyu
  1½ Tbsp. garlic granules or 5 garlic cloves, minced or
    pressed

Mix water, shoyu and garlic, and pour over tofu slices arranged on a baking pan. Bake at 350°F until tofu is firm and liquid is absorbed, approximately ½ hour.

Tips:

– Recipe can be reduced.

– Tofu keeps longer this way than when plain. This will keep for 7-8 days and becomes "cheesier" as it ages.

– For sandwiches, slice and roll up thin pieces of Garlic Tofu in nori sushi-rolls with carrots, scallions and ginger pickles, or serve on crackers with cucumber slices.

Baked Cheesy Tofu

24 oz. tofu
2 Tbsp. white or yellow miso
1 cup water
2 to 3 Tbsp. tahini or sesame butter
6 oz. mugwort mochi, grated or minced finely

Cut tofu in 2" x 1" x ¼" pieces. Arrange on a 9" x 18" baking pan.

Make a sauce by diluting miso in water; add tahini and mochi bits and mix well. Pour sauce over tofu and bake, uncovered, at 350°F for 15 to 25 minutes, until it has a cheesy, baked-on appearance and is lightly browned. Serves 6.

Serving Suggestions:

– Serve with steamed kale with sauerkraut, baked squash or long-cooked carrots with parsley, brown rice, rice and barley, or udon noodles.

Tofu Lasagna

Great to make ahead for a quick meal.

4 cups minced white onion
1 Tbsp. sesame oil
2 pounds tofu, crumbled
½ cup water
2 Tbsp. shoyu
8 long strips whole wheat spinach lasagna noodles
1 recipe Tomato-Less Sauce (page 58)
½ to ¾ cup grated mochi
¼ cup tahini
2 Tbsp. white or yellow miso
1¼ cups water

Saute onion in oil for 3 to 4 minutes. Add tofu. Mix water and shoyu and add to onion and tofu mixture. Stir over medium heat 5 minutes, then turn off heat and set aside.

Cook noodles in a large pot of boiling water until almost soft – al dente. Rinse with cold water to prevent sticking.

Lightly oil a 9" x 14" x 2" lasagna pan. Place one layer of noodles to cover the bottom. Spoon 2½ cups tomato-less sauce over noodles. Spread 4 cups tofu mixture on top. Cover with another layer of noodles. Spoon remaining sauce over noodles, followed by remaining tofu mixture. Top with grated mochi.

Mix tahini, miso, and water; pour over lasagna. Cover and bake 30 to 40 minutes, then remove cover and bake 15 minutes or until golden on top.

If you are making this ahead, assemble lasagna and refrigerate until ready to bake, or bake covered 30 minutes then refrigerate and reheat when ready to use.

Tofu Corn Tortilla Scramble

3 cups onions, chopped
1½ Tbsp. sesame, safflower, or corn oil
1½ lbs. tofu, crumbled
1½ to 2 Tbsp. shoyu
1½ tsp. cumin
6 to 8 corn tortillas
water

Saute onions in oil until translucent, approximately 5 minutes. Add tofu, shoyu, and cumin and stir.

Tear corn tortillas into pieces and combine with onion and tofu mixture. Add 2 to 3 tablespoons water and cook over medium heat for 5 minutes.

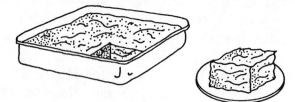

Tips:

– For best flavor, bake this dish as a casserole: add ½ cup water, pour into a casserole dish and bake at 325°F for 20 to 30 minutes or until set. Slice in squares.

– Garnish with minced parsley or scallions and serve with steamed greens, sauerkraut, and baked squash, with or without brown rice.

Tofu Cheese

≡ 1 lb. firm or medium tofu
3 to 6 Tbsp. barley miso or soybean miso
water

Rinse tofu; slice into 4 layers. Mix miso with enough water to make a spreadable paste. Spread miso on the top, sides, and between each layer of tofu. Cover with a plate. It will look like a layered chocolate cake while it's aging.

Keep it refrigerated for 2 to 6 days. The tofu becomes more cheesy the longer it sits. Scrape off excess miso from tofu before using it. Save miso to season beans or soup.

Serving Suggestions:

– Add tofu cheese to a stir fry, omitting shoyu.

– Bake, steam, or lightly saute tofu cheese slices for several minutes with or without chopped onions and mushrooms. Serve over brown rice with lotus seeds or over noodles. Top with crumbled roasted nori, if desired.

– Good side dishes with cooked tofu cheese:
- boiled kale or steamed broccoli served with toasted sesame seeds;
- delicatta squash rings;
- arame seaweed or roasted sheet of nori seaweed crumbled on top.

Tofu Cheese Scramble

1 to 2 tsp. sesame oil
1 large onion, cut into thin half-moon pieces
dash water
¼ to ⅓ lb. Tofu Cheese (page 99)
water
1 or 2 sheets nori seaweed

Lightly oil skillet, then add onions and saute until onions are translucent. Crumble tofu cheese into onions. Add water a tablespoon at a time to keep scramble moist.

Toast a sheet or two of nori and cut or crumble it into the pan. Cook and scramble 5 minutes.

Serving Suggestions:

– Serve over noodles or rice with steamed greens and carrots or squash.

Lotus Root with Tofu Cheese
Has a cheesy and potato taste and is very nourishing.

Tofu Cheese (page 99)
2, 4-inch pieces fresh lotus root

Cut fresh lotus root in ¼-inch to ⅓-inch slices. Steam 25 minutes or until tender.

Bake, broil, or steam tofu cheese for 8 to 10 minutes. Place tofu cheese slices on top of cooked lotus root.

Serving Suggestions:

– Serve with udon noodles, rice, rice and wheat, or rice and lotus seeds, and steamed broccoli, carrots, or squash.

Tofu French Toast

1½ cups tofu
¼ tsp. cinnamon
¼ cup or less rice syrup
¼ to ½ tsp. sea salt
½ cup water
2 Tbsp. oil

Blend all ingredients in a blender until smooth and creamy and pour into a shallow bowl.

Dip slices of day-old wholegrain bread in batter, then fry on a lightly oiled hot skillet. Brown well on both sides.

Serve with warm rice syrup and chopped roasted pecans, or maple syrup, or applesauce. Makes 8 slices.

Tofu Enchiladas

A rich, cheesy dish without
the cholesterol or calories.

3 lbs. tofu, frozen, thawed, and torn into bite-sized
    pieces
2 Tbsp. peanut butter or sesame butter
1 tsp. cumin
2 Tbsp. shoyu
2 Tbsp. water
¼ to ½ cup oil
16 to 18 stoneground corn tortillas

Blenderize nut butter, cumin, shoyu, and water. Mix with
tofu and saute in oil in a cast iron skillet, stirring well, until
browned. Set aside.

Mild Chili Gravy:

2 medium-sized onions, minced
2 Tbsp. light sesame, corn, or safflower oil
1 tsp. cumin
¼ to ½ tsp. sea salt
1 tsp. garlic powder
1 to 2 Tbsp. chili powder (to taste)
4 Tbsp. rice flour or 2 Tbsp. kuzu or arrowroot dissolved in
    cold water
2 to 5 cups water

Saute onions in oil until soft. Add cumin, salt, garlic powder,
chili powder, and flour or kuzu or arrowroot. Stir well and
add water. Whip slowly to prevent lumps from forming.
Bring to a boil, then simmer over medium heat 20 minutes.

Topping:

≡
⫴   1 to 1½ cups minced onion (optional)
⫴   1 to 1½ cups chopped black olives (optional)
≡   1 to 1½ cups grated mochi

Assembling:

Place ⅓ to ½ cup browned tofu mixture on a corn tortilla, and roll it up. Continue process until tofu mixture is used up. Pour a thin layer of chili gravy on the bottom of a 9" x 14" x 2" baking pan. Arrange rolled tortillas, tightly packed, in pan. Pour remaining gravy over tortillas. Extra gravy may be saved for another use. Sprinkle with topping. Cover and bake at 350°F for 10 to 15 minutes, or uncovered until mochi bubbles and turns golden. Serves 8 to 10.

Variations and Serving Suggestions:

– For a milder and quicker dish, omit chili gravy and re-place it with the following sauce:

  4 to 6 Tbsp. tahini
  3 to 4 tsp. white miso
  2½ to 3 cups water
  1 tsp. garlic powder
  1 tsp. cumin (optional)

Mix tahini, miso, and water. Add seasonings to taste. Pour this cheesy sauce over rolled up tortillas and top with 1½ to 2 cups grated mochi. Bake at 350°F, covered or uncovered, for 15 minutes.

– Serve with:

  - Brown rice, steamed kale, broccoli, carrots, or boiled salad;
  - Boiled corn on the cob and a gelled fruit dessert.

Grains and Noodles

Brown Rice

Brown rice can be boiled, pressure cooked, baked, roasted, or fried. Pressure cooking is a desirable method because nutrients are retained in the rice, not boiled away. For many people pressure-cooked rice is easier to digest and tastes better than boiled rice. Use a stainless steel or enamel pressure cooker rather than an aluminum one.

To Pressure Cook:

2 cups brown rice
2¾ to 3 cups water
2 pinches sea salt

Wash rice three times, drain, then add fresh water and salt. Put lid on cooker, and turn burner to highest setting.

When the valve pops, jiggles, or whistles, turn heat to low. Use a flame deflector if using a gas stove.

Cook 45 to 50 minutes. Remove from heat and allow pressure to come down.

To Boil:

2 cups brown rice
4 cups water
2 pinches sea salt

Wash rice three times and drain. In a heavy saucepan, bring water, rice, and salt to a boil. Cover, turn burner to low heat, and simmer for 1 hour. Do not stir the rice during this time.

Turn off heat and let rice sit 10 to 15 minutes.

Tips and Variations:

– Remove rice from the pan with a wooden spoon by taking pie-shaped pieces from the top and bottom and spreading rice in a large wooden, glass, or pottery bowl. Separate the grains with a rice paddle. Do this for the whole pot to prevent gummy, mushy rice.

– The amount of water and time of cooking may vary with the amount of rice cooked, altitude, weather, temperature, etc.

– For a more robust-flavored rice, cook in bancha tea or roasted barley tea instead of water. Season before cooking with a pinch of salt per cup of rice.

– Sea salt in the correct proportion does not make the rice salty; rather, it helps alkalinize the grain so it will digest more easily. You can occasionally substitute the following condiments for salt:

    - shoyu, 1 or 2 teaspoons per pot;
    - umeboshi plums, 1 or 2 plums per pot;
    - takuan pickle;
    - shiso leaves or shiso powder.

– Leftover rice may be kept up to 3 days at room temperature in a cool climate or season. Refrigeration may cause the rice to dry out and lose its flavor, while rice kept at room temperature improves in flavor if it was cooked with sea salt.

Rice Kayu Cereal (Rice Cream)

≡ 1 cup brown rice
1 cup sweet brown rice
6 cups water
2 pinches sea salt

Wash rice. Combine ingredients and pressure cook 45 to 50 minutes. Eat as is, or press through a sieve to produce a creamier consistency. Use the leftover bran in cookies or breads.

Serve with applesauce, apple butter, tekka, or gomashio.

Wheat Berry Rice

≡ ¼ cup wheat berries, washed and soaked overnight
1 cup short-grain brown rice
1½ to 1¾ cups water for pressure-cooked rice; (2 to 2½ cups for boiled rice)
1 pinch sea salt

Drain soaked wheat berries, and wash rice. Cook grains in water and salt according to directions for Brown Rice.

Leftover wheat berry rice takes on a sourdough-like flavor as it ages. Cover it with a bamboo sushi mat. One- or two-day-old wheat berry rice is easier to digest and has a nice sour taste. Pan-fry it by sauteing chopped celery, carrot, and scallion, then adding wheat berry rice, a dash of shoyu and roasted pumpkin seeds if desired. Or make patties from day-old wheat berry rice and pan-fry, topping patties with gravy.

Variations:

– Sprouted Wheat and Rice: Soak wheat berries overnight, then rinse daily for 3 to 4 days or until sprouts form. Cook as for Wheat Berry Rice.

– Rye Berry Rice: Tastes like rye bread. Soak rye berries overnight and cook as for Wheat Berry Rice.

– Barley Rice: A slightly sweet, chewy combination. Use the same proportions as for Wheat Berry Rice.

– Oat Groat Rice: Soak ¼ cup oat groats overnight. Boil with ¾ cup brown rice or pressure cook with 1 cup brown rice.

– Hato Mugi Rice: Soak ¼ cup hato mugi grain for several hours or overnight, then cook with 1 cup brown rice.

– Millet Rice: Combine grains using your own preference for proportions. Try half millet, half brown rice. Cook as for Wheat Berry Rice.

Brown Rice with Sweet Rice and Almonds

2 cups sweet brown rice
2 cups short-grain brown rice
1 cup almonds, halved or whole
¼ tsp. sea salt
6 cups water

Wash rice. Pressure cook with almonds, sea salt, and water for 50 to 55 minutes.

Tips:

– You may substitute chopped walnuts, or soaked dried chestnuts, or whole, peeled peanuts for almonds.

– This dish is great with baked or nishime style root vegetables like onions, squash, carrots, turnips or rutabagas. Steamed greens or a boiled salad with sauerkraut round out this meal, with or without miso soup and a sea vegetable condiment.

Variations:

– 2 cups brown rice, 2 cups barley, 1 cup sesame seeds, 6 cups water and ¼ tsp. sea salt.

– 3 cups brown rice, ⅔ cups pine nuts, 4 cups water, and ¼ tsp. sea salt.

– 3 cups brown rice, ½ cup wild rice, ½ cup pecans, 5¾ cups water, and ¼ tsp. sea salt.

– 2 cups brown rice, 2 cups millet, 1 cup sesame seeds, 6 cups water, and ¼ tsp. sea salt.

– 2 cups brown rice, 2 cups quinoa, 6 cups water, and ¼ tsp. sea salt.

– 3 cups brown rice, 1 cup amaranth (or 2 cups brown rice, 2 cups amaranth), 6 cups water, and ¼ tsp. sea salt.

– 2 cups millet, 2 cups sweet brown rice, ½ cup walnuts, 6 cups water, and ¼ tsp. sea salt.

Lotus Rice

¾ cup dry lotus seed halves
3 to 4 cups water
4 cups short-grain brown rice, washed
6-inch piece fresh lotus root, scrubbed well and cut into thin
   rounds
½ tsp. plus 2 pinches sea salt
6¼ cups water

Soak lotus seeds overnight in 3 to 4 cups water. In the morning throw out the soak water. Place rinsed lotus seeds, rice, lotus root pieces, salt, and 6¼ cups water in a pressure cooker; bring to full pressure. Pressure cook 50 to 60 minutes.

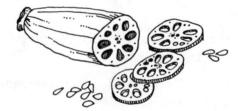

Lotus and Shiitake Rice

¼ cup dried lotus root, soaked several hours
¼ cup dried lotus seeds, soaked all day or overnight
4 dried shiitake mushrooms, soaked and cut finely
2 cups short-grain brown rice, washed
3 to 3¼ cups water
4 pinches sea salt

Combine all ingredients and pressure cook 45 to 50 minutes. For variation, add ½ cup uncooked squash, cubed.

Lotus Seed Rice

¼ cup dried lotus seeds, soaked overnight
2 cups brown rice, washed
3 cups water
4 pinches sea salt

Combine all ingredients and pressure cook for 50 minutes.

Variations:

– Rice with Sunnies: Add ⅓ to ½ cup sunflower seeds to 2 cups brown rice before cooking, and use shoyu instead of sea salt. Or roast sunflower seeds while rice is cooking, then toss them together while both are still warm.

– Rice with Walnuts or Almonds: Roast chopped walnuts or almonds while brown rice is cooking. When rice is done, remove some of it with a wooden paddle into a large wooden bowl or glass casserole dish. Add a thin layer of nuts, then repeat until all the rice is removed from the pot.

– Rice and Sesame: Cook ½ cup black sesame seeds with 2 cups brown rice for an attractive and flavorful combination.

– Rice with Dried Chestnuts: Soak ¼ cup dried chestnuts. Cook with 2 cups brown rice using soaking water as part of liquid.

Tofu Rice

¼ cup tofu, crumbled
sesame oil
1 cup short-grain brown rice, washed
¼ tsp. shoyu
1¼ to 1½ cups water

Pan-fry tofu bits in a dash of sesame oil. Combine with remaining ingredients and pressure cook for 45 to 50 minutes.

Variations:

– Seitan can be used in place of tofu.

– Sauteed onion, carrot, and burdock slivers can be added with tofu or seitan and pressure cooked with the rice.

Rice with Beans

The amounts can be changed as long as you keep in mind these proportions:

⅛ to ¼ cup dry beans
6-inch piece kombu seaweed (optional)
1 cup brown rice, washed
2 pinches sea salt
2 to 2½ cups water

Soak azuki beans, black soybeans, chickpeas, pinto beans, or other beans 5 to 6 hours or overnight. Drain beans. Bring to a boil with kombu and water.

Add rice and sea salt. Add more water if necessary. Cover and simmer 45 to 50 minutes (50 to 60 minutes for black soybeans or chickpeas), then let cool 10 to 15 minutes.

Variations:

– To pressure cook, use 1¾ cups water and pressure cook 45 to 50 minutes.

– Try other grain and bean combinations:
- pinto beans with barley or brown rice;
- azukis or black beans with sweet brown rice;
- chickpeas with barley or barley and brown rice;
- lentils with brown rice and sunflower seeds.

Sushi

Japanese tradition . . . American ease. You will need:

bamboo sushi mat
1 chopstick
sushi nori
1½ cups sticky rice
sesame butter or tahini
pickled ginger
cooked carrot strips

Sticky Rice:

3 cups uncooked brown rice
4 cups water
3 pinches sea salt
2 Tbsp. ume vinegar (optional)

Wash rice. Place rice, water, and salt in pressure cooker and cook for 50 minutes. Remove rice to a bowl and add ume vinegar. Gently mix, separating the grains of rice. Allow to cool.

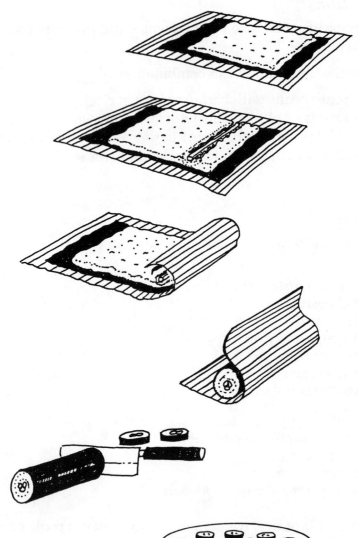

Carrot strips:

Cut carrots into strips ¼-inch thick and wide. Boil in water with a pinch of salt for 1 to 2 minutes. Set aside.

Assembling sushi:

Lay bamboo mat with bamboo grain running left/right. Place one piece of sushi nori on mat as pictured.

Wet hands with water. Press approximately ½ cup of rice onto sushi nori. Leave 1 inch at top and bottom of nori uncovered. Try to press rice on evenly and all the way to the sides of the nori.

Lay chopstick on rice 1 inch from the edge of rice nearest to you. Press chopstick into rice to make an indentation just deep enough to hold fillings. Fill indentation with one line of carrot strips, one line of pickled ginger, and one line of sesame butter.

Rolling sushi:

Starting from the edge nearest to you, roll up mat around ingredients. Press firmly as you roll. As you are rolling, pull leading edge of mat away from sushi to avoid getting mat stuck in the sushi. Continue rolling until you reach the end of the nori.

Moisten the edge of the nori with a little water. Complete rolling and give a final gentle squeeze to seal sushi. Remove sushi mat. Continue making sushi rolls as described.

Run a knife under cold water, then gently cut each sushi roll in half. Cut each half in half, and so on to make 8 slices or until slices are the width you like.

Stuffed Grape Leaves
Great for parties.

- 5 cups cooked long-grain brown rice
- 2 to 4 Tbsp. olive oil
- 4 cloves garlic, minced
- 1 large onion, minced
- ¼ cup shoyu
- ¾ cup sunflower seeds, toasted
- 1 tsp. basil
- 1 tsp. thyme
- 3 Tbsp. ao-nori flakes
- 1 jar (8 ounces) grape leaves
- juice of 1 lemon

Heat oil and saute garlic until browned. Add onion; saute until translucent. Add cooked rice and stir. Add shoyu, sunflower seeds, basil, thyme, and ao-nori flakes; stir well.

Rinse grape leaves well. Fill each grape leaf with 2 tablespoons rice mixture: Spread leaf out, place filling in the middle, fold right side in, bottom piece up. Fold left side in, and roll up. Place finished rolls in a baking dish. This should make 40 stuffed rolls.

Squeeze lemon juice over entire batch of stuffed grape leaves, if desired, and serve warmed or at room temperature. These keep well in airtight containers in the refrigerator.

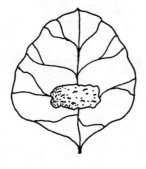

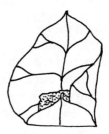

Other Whole Grains

Quick-n-Easy Millet Squares

2 cups millet, rinsed in a sieve
6 cups water
3 pinches sea salt
4 carrots, cut in tiny pieces
1½ cups fresh parsley, rinsed well, cut finely
1½ to 1¾ cups sunflower seeds, roasted

Bring rinsed millet, water, and salt to boil. Cover and simmer over low heat 40 to 45 minutes. Turn off heat and let it sit 5 to 10 minutes.

Steam carrot pieces 3 to 5 minutes or blanch in boiling water 1 to 2 minutes. Mix carrots, parsley, sunflower seeds, and warm millet. Press into 9" x 13" x 2" pan. Let cool until set, then slice into 3-inch squares.

Variations:

– Add steamed cauliflower, celery, or scallion to cooked millet and sunflower seeds.

– Add sauteed carrot matchsticks, minced celery, and minced onion.

– Add sauteed kale, carrot, and onion.

– Add cooked hijiki seaweed with any of the vegetables for a colorful, mineral-rich dish.

– Top with Mustard and Mayo Sauce.

Millet Mound

2 cups millet, rinsed in a sieve
1 head cauliflower, cut into small florets
5½ cups water
2 pinches sea salt

Bring ingredients to a boil in a covered pot. Simmer over low heat 45 to 50 minutes. Let sit 5 to 10 minutes to steam in pot.

Spoon into large bundt cake pan and press firmly to fill in edges. Let cool to set. Turn out onto serving plate.

Serving Suggestions:

– Cut into slices and top with Walnut Miso Gravy. Garnish with fresh parsley.

– This is great for breakfast made into a porridge with umeboshi plum or shiso leaf condiment sprinkled on top, or lightly pan-fried in slices.

Millet Tabouli Salad

3 Tbsp. light sesame oil, toasted sesame oil, or olive oil
5 cloves fresh garlic, minced
4 to 5 stalks celery
¾ cup roasted walnuts, sunflower seeds, or pine nuts, chopped
5 to 6 cups freshly cooked or leftover millet, or brown rice
½ cup fresh parsley, chopped
1 Tbsp. umeboshi vinegar
1 Tbsp. oregano
1 Tbsp. dill weed

Place oil in heated skillet. Add minced garlic and saute 2 to 3 minutes. Add celery and saute 1 to 2 minutes. Add 2 to 3 teaspoons of water to moisten; then add chopped nuts. Mix in millet, stir, then add parsley. Stir gently with chopsticks or a wooden spoon, and turn off heat. Add vinegar and adjust seasoning if necessary.

Serve with lemon slices for a zesty garnish.

Stuffed Mock Grape Leaves

Blanch collard greens or other large leafy greens in boiling water for 2 minutes. Remove from water and allow to cool, then lay each leaf on a flat surface. Cut out a "V" shape where the stem is thick and remove the piece. Place 2 tablespoons of Millet Tabouli in the middle of the leaf. Tuck in the sides of the leaf to cover the Tabouli, then fold up the bottom edge and roll the pouch away from you. Do this with all the remaining leaves.

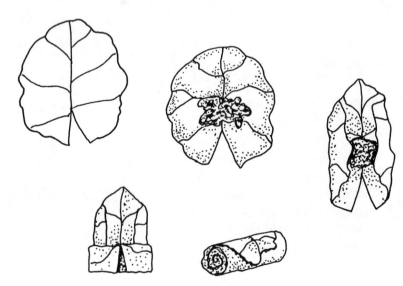

Place the stuffed green leaves on a baking dish and drizzle with a mixture of lemon juice and olive oil, using 1½ tablespoons lemon juice or rice vinegar and 1½ tablespoons oil per 24 rolls. Bake in an uncovered baking dish for 10 to 12 minutes or until warm.

Stuffed Mock Grape Leaves make great hors d'oeuvres, snacks, lunch box treats, or meal mates with soup and chickpea pate or hummus.

Millet Stuffing

3 cups millet, rinsed in a sieve
5 cups boiling water
½ tsp. sea salt
1 tsp. sesame oil
1 medium onion, sliced or chopped
3 carrots, cut into matchstick pieces
greens from 1 head cauliflower, cut finely
2 to 3 stalks celery
½ cup fresh parsley, chopped
dash shoyu
½ cup walnuts or sunflower seeds, roasted and chopped
    (optional)
2 to 3 tsp. juice squeezed from 1 handful grated ginger

Roast millet in a dry skillet until it has a nutty aroma. Stir gently to prevent it from burning. Add millet to boiling water and salt. Cover, bring to a boil, then reduce heat and cook 25 to 30 minutes.

Brush skillet with sesame oil. Saute onion until translucent, then add carrots, greens, celery, and parsley. Add a small amount of water if necessary to prevent scorching. Season with shoyu. Add millet, walnuts or sunflower seeds, if desired, and ginger juice.

Serving suggestions:

– Fill centers of Delicatta Squash Rings and arrange on platter.

– Blanch cabbage or collard leaves and roll a spoonful of stuffing in each leaf. Serve with a slice of lemon and a sprig of parsley.

Millet Loaf

1 cup millet, rinsed in a sieve
1 to 2 cups cut cauliflower
1 Tbsp. white or mellow miso
3 cups water

Pressure cook all ingredients 15 to 18 minutes. Turn off heat and reduce pressure right away to prevent bitterness. Spoon into loaf pan and let set. Turn out on a serving platter and cut in slices.

Serving suggestions:

– Serve with:

- steamed broccoli;
- steamed kale tossed with a dash of natural sauerkraut;
- baked squash or boiled squash;
- steamed or blanched carrot pieces with minced parsley.

– Pan-fry slices and serve with steamed vegetables.

– Serve as millet "mashed potatoes": Add 2 to 3 Tbsp. tahini to hot millet mixture and stir well.

– Add ½ tsp. basil and thyme combined, or dill and chives combined.

– Form cooked millet mixture into balls and roll in toasted sesame seeds.

– Serve hot millet mixture for breakfast with toasted sesame seeds sprinkled on top.

Millet Rye Berry Loaf

3 cups millet
1 cup rye berries
7 cups water
2 pinches sea salt

Rinse and roast the two grains separately in a cast iron skillet or a stainless steel pot. Add water and salt, bring to a boil, reduce heat, and simmer over low heat for 45 minutes. Then press into two loaf pans or one large baking pan. Let cool until set, then slice.

Serving suggestions:

– Good with a gravy or a tahini sauce. Try Sesame Sauce with Thyme or Sunflower Basil Sauce.

– Pan-fry slices and top with grated daikon, shoyu, and scallions.

Sweet Rice and Millet Balls

1 cup millet, rinsed in a sieve
2 cups sweet brown rice, washed
4 cups water
½ tsp. sea salt
1 cup sesame seeds, sunflower seeds, almonds, or walnuts
1½ tsp. sea salt

Pressure cook millet, rice, water, and ½ teaspoon salt 45 to 50 minutes.

Meanwhile, make a gomashio-type mixture of seeds or nuts and salt: Roast 1½ teaspoon salt and grind in a suribachi. Roast seeds or nuts. Gently grind with salt.

Remove millet and rice from pressure cooker. Allow to cool slightly. With wet hands, form millet rice mixture into small balls and roll in seed or nut mixture.

Whole Oat Porridge
Very warming for winter mornings.

1 cup whole oat groats, washed and soaked overnight or for
    4 to 5 hours
4½ cups water
1 to 2 pinches sea salt

Cook ingredients over low heat for 3 hours, or cook over-night with two flame tamers under the pot and using the lowest setting possible on the stove.

Variations:

– Soak oats and before cooking add ¼ cup each: chopped almonds, sunflower seeds, raisins. Cook as directed above.

– Soak ¼ to ½ cup lotus seeds with the oats, and cook as instructed, using 4 cups water.

– Soak ¼ cup dried chestnuts with the oats and cook as above.

– Add 1 to 2 cups cubed winter squash during the last 1 to 2 hours of cooking. Toast 1 to 2 sheets nori over an open flame or burner, then cut into very thin strips for a garnish.

Oats Deluxe

3 to 3½ cups water
1 pinch sea salt
1½ cups rolled oats

Bring ingredients to a boil. Do not stir. Cover, turn burner to low heat, and simmer for 20 to 25 minutes.

Serving variations:

– Sprinkle roasted sesame seeds or tekka over servings.

– Top with chopped raisins, roasted sunflower seeds or almonds, and tekka.

– Top with roasted pumpkin seeds and sprinkle with shiso

leaf powder.

– Serve with baked or pureed squash, carrot butter, or onion butter on the side.

– Mix leftover cooked squash with rolled oats, then add more water and cook 30 minutes. Add strips of toasted nori seaweed or sprinkle with tekka condiment.

– Add raisins and/or cinnamon to oatmeal and squash mixture.

Mirin Oat Biscuits

5 cups rolled oats
⅓ cup cold-pressed corn oil
1 cup mirin
¾ cup water
⅓ cup sunflower seeds

Mix ingredients together. Shape into 3-inch round biscuits, about ⅓-inch thick, on a lightly oiled baking pan. Bake at 350°F about 20 minutes, or until golden brown.

Granola

4 cups rolled oats, or mixed flaked grains (oat flakes, barley flakes, rye flakes)
½ cup whole wheat flour
1 tsp. cinnamon
½ tsp. nutmeg
¼ cup almonds, sunflower seeds, or walnuts
⅓ cup rice syrup
1 Tbsp. barley malt

Mix all ingredients and bake at 400°F for 20 minutes on lightly oiled sheet, stirring every 5 minutes or so.

Grain Patties

½ cup dry bulgur
½ tsp. sea salt
¾ cup water
2 Tbsp. shoyu
⅓ block firm tofu or tempeh, crumbled
½ cup chopped onion
¼ tsp. thyme
1 tsp. grated ginger
1 tsp. sesame oil
1 tsp. kuzu powder or arrowroot powder
¼ cup chopped filberts or walnuts
¼ cup raw sunflower seeds
Onion Gravy (page 166)

Combine bulgur, salt, water, and shoyu. Bring to a boil, then
simmer over low heat 20 minutes until liquid is absorbed.

Mix bulgur with other ingredients, making sure tofu or
tempeh is well crumbled. Form into patties and fry on oiled
griddle at medium heat for 2 minutes each side.

Serve with onion gravy. Serves 3.

Stuffed Mushroom Caps

2 tsp. toasted sesame oil
1 onion, minced
3 stalks celery, minced
1 cup bulgur wheat
2 handfuls chopped pecans or walnuts
2 pinches sea salt
1½ cups water
1½ Tbsp. bancha tea or barley tea
⅓ cup water
20 to 25 large cap mushrooms with center core removed
dash basil, thyme, or seaweed powder
dash shoyu

Heat skillet; add oil and saute onion 3 minutes or until translucent. Add celery, bulgur, chopped nuts, and 1½ cups water and tea. Stir, reduce heat to low, and saute 10 minutes or until liquid is absorbed. Add herbs during last few minutes of cooking.

Fill mushroom caps with stuffing, packed in well. Place on baking pans with about ⅓-inch water in bottom of pan. Bake at 350°F for 1 hour or until mushrooms are brown and liquid is absorbed.

Mochi

Marvelous Mochi

Frozen or dried mochi can be used to make delicious toast-like squares without flour, wheat, yeast, or other ingredients. Mochi is made from sweet rice which has been cooked and pounded. It is thought to be strengthening and good for the intestines.

Mochi comes in many varieties. Frozen mochi is available in cinnamon, raisin, plain, organic, garlic, sesame, and mugwort (a green herb high in iron, calcium, and other minerals). Frozen mochi tends to be fresher tasting than dried mochi. It comes in a large block, usually 12.5 ounces. Dried mochi in the following varieties: brown rice, millet, mugwort, sesame and rice, comes in 10.5-ounce packages, six squares per package.

You can use mochi puffs like croutons to be dropped in soup, to toss into vegetable salads with hummus (chickpea dip), or a tofu cream cheese or tofu sauce, to serve as dessert with toppings, or for breakfast. Some people who try mochi find it too gooey and glutinous. Try the recipes for mochi toast which tastes like real toast but is much more nourishing and less mucus producing than bread and flour products.

Mochi Oven Toast

For each person, cut two squares of dried mochi into 9 to 12 smaller cubes. Or cut frozen mochi into ½-inch cubes. Arrange on a dry cookie sheet or other non-glass pan. Bake at

400° to 450°F for 10 to 12 minutes or until puffy and slightly golden. Serve while warm.

Serving Suggestions:

- Toast one sheet of nori seaweed per person, then break or cut it into long strips. Grate daikon radish very finely; drizzle a dash of shoyu over it. Wrap a strip of nori over a mochi cube, and spoon on a dash of daikon.

- Drizzle brown rice syrup or tahini and rice syrup over mochi cubes for a sweet treat.

- Serve mochi puffs with leftover steamed vegies and a tofu sauce or dip.

- Drop mochi puffs in your miso soup as croutons.

- Roll each cube in rice malt, then in kinako (toasted soybean flour, available in most Japanese or macrobiotic stores) for a nice, rich, nutty taste.

- Bake cinnamon raisin mochi on a dry sheet and serve with a dab of tahini or sesame butter and rice malt syrup. Tastes like cinnamon toast.

- Serve baked mochi puffs with cooked wakame and lotus seeds on a bed of cooked kale.

- Serve baked mochi puffs with a pressed salad of cucumber, radish, carrot slivers and soaked wakame massaged with salt, pressed several hours and rinsed.

- Stuff baked toast cubes with Whole Lotus Seeds.

- Fill baked cubes with rice malt, Chestnut Puree, or sesame butter and malt syrup. Serve warm as a dessert or breakfast treat.

Mochi Skillet Toast

Allow 4 ounces dried mochi per person.

Place approximately 2 to 3 teaspoons toasted sesame oil in a cast iron skillet. Cut mochi into ½- to ¾-inch cubes and place in skillet, first on high temperature, then medium. As each side gets done, turn it over using chopsticks, so each of the six sides gets browned; this will take 4 to 8 minutes. Keep watching and turning to prevent burning. The skillet will dry out as oil is absorbed, but continue to dry roast until mochi is puffy.

Serving suggestions:

– Roll each cube in kinako (roasted soybean flour), then wrap with toasted nori. Pop each bit into your mouth with a piece of sushi ginger pickle or the shiso leaf from a package of sushi ginger pickles. It is also good with steamed kale.

– Roll each piece in rice syrup and kinako powder or roasted almond, walnut, or pecan meal.

– Wrap in tiny pieces of pickled shiso leaf (from your umeboshi plum jar) and strips of toasted nori seaweed.

– For a summer salad, use olive oil to saute or pan-roast garlic sesame mochi and toss into steamed vegie salads with or without tofu sauce or dip.

Noodles

Noodles are more digestible than bread or hard baked flour products, which are more acid-forming in the stomach. This does not mean such flour products as bread and pastries should not be eaten — it just means they should not make up the bulk of our meals. Flour products can best be used as occasional additions to meals, as snacks or desserts.

Of all flour products, noodles seem to be the easiest to digest. Japanese whole wheat udon noodles are easier to digest than whole wheat noodles made from durum wheat. Several varieties of Japanese noodles are:

– Buckwheat soba (100 percent buckwheat, wheat-free; or 40 percent buckwheat, 60 percent sifted wheat);

– Lotus root soba (buckwheat and lotus root);

– Mugwort soba (buckwheat and mugwort leaf);

– Jinenjo soba (mountain yam, buckwheat, and whole wheat);

– Whole wheat udon (100 percent whole wheat; or partially sifted);

– Brown rice udon (light noodle; brown rice and wheat).

Other types of Japanese noodles are used in macrobiotic cookery, but these are the most common. They can be served hot or cold, in salads, in soups and broths, or stir-fried with vegetables.

American elbow macaroni, ziti noodles and other shapes can be used in casseroles, lasagna, salads, and ethnic dishes. Brown rice elbow macaroni, corn noodles, spinach noodles, pasta shells and others can be used occasionally.

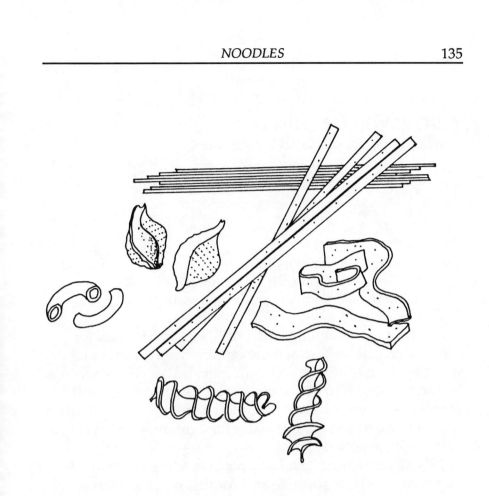

To cook udon and soba noodles:

Most udon and soba noodles are already salted, so they are boiled in unsalted water. Shock noodles by adding cold water when they first come to a boil. Repeat this 3 to 5 times until the noodles test done. This prevents soggy noodles and aids in even cooking. Total boiling time is 8 to 10 minutes. Noodles are done when the color on the outside and inside is the same, and when the noodles taste done. If the noodles are not to be used immediately, rinse with cold water to prevent sticking.

Corn Noodle Salad
A wheat-free noodle salad for summer.

- 1 lb. (16-oz. package) corn spaghetti
- 2 leeks
- 4 to 5 carrots
- 1½ Tbsp. umeboshi vinegar
- 1½ Tbsp. water
- 1½ Tbsp. corn oil or safflower oil
- 2 to 3 tsp. shiso leaf sprinkle (optional)
- ⅓ cup roasted pumpkin seeds (optional)

Cook spaghetti in boiling water until tender; rinse under cold water. Cut leeks down the center, then run under cold water to clean sand out, separating the leaves with your hands. Cut into thin half-moon pieces. Scrub carrots well and cut into thin half-moon or quarter-moon pieces. Blanch leeks and carrots in boiling water for 2 minutes, then remove pieces with a slotted spoon.

Mix all ingredients well and place in a large serving bowl. Top with shiso leaf sprinkle and roasted pumpkin seeds, if desired. Serve, or cover and chill. Serves 6 to 8.

Noodle Salad with Chickpeas

- 1 cup chickpeas, cooked with sea salt
- 4 cups cooked noodles (whole wheat spinach noodles, or rice or wheat noodles, or vegetable noodles, or pasta shells)

Mash half of the chickpeas. Mix with noodles. Use one of the following dressings.

Lime Dressing:

2 Tbsp. fresh lime juice
½ tsp. basil
½ tsp. dill
3 Tbsp. olive oil
1 Tbsp. ume vinegar
1 clove garlic, minced or pressed

Shake all ingredients in a bottle. Add to noodles and chick-peas. Serve cold.

Vinaigrette:

4 Tbsp. olive oil
2 tsp. prepared mustard
1 Tbsp. vinegar
minced celery

Shake all ingredients in a bottle. Add to noodles and chick-peas. Serve cold.

Curry Dressing:

sesame butter
shoyu or white miso
cumin
curry powder
dash of rice vinegar

Add ingredients to warm noodles and chickpeas. Serve warm.

Jinenjo Soba Salad

1 cup slivered almonds
3 cups cooked jinenjo soba noodles or udon
1 to 2 Tbsp. olive oil
1 or more cloves garlic, pressed (optional)
½ cup parsley, chopped
1 cup cooked chickpeas
¼ to ⅓ cup green ao-nori flakes
¼ cup Toasted Wakame Powder (page 184)

Toast almond pieces in a dry skillet until light brown. Stir
with wooden spoon to turn and prevent burning.

Rinse cooked noodles with cold water to prevent sticking.
Drain well. Heat oil in pan and saute garlic 2 to 3 minutes.
Turn off heat and add parsley and noodles. Stir. Add chick-
peas, ao-nori flakes, and wakame powder. Mix in almonds.

Refrigerate leftover salad.

Udon Boiled Salad

8 oz. udon noodles, cooked
¼ to 1 head cauliflower, cut into florets and steamed or
    blanched
3 to 4 finely cut leeks, blanched 1 minute
½ cup cooked arame or hijiki seaweed (optional)

Place noodles in individual bowls. If using arame or hijiki,
layer it over noodles. Layer cooked cauliflower and leeks on
top. Top with Mirin-Sesame Dressing or Pumpkin or Sunflower Seed Dressings. Serves 4.

Mirin Sesame Dressing:

2 Tbsp. mirin
3 to 4 Tbsp. brown rice vinegar
1 to 2 Tbsp. light miso
½ to ¾ cup sesame seeds, roasted and ground
⅓ to ⅔ cup hot or warm water, to taste

Mix or mash ingredients with fork, or whisk and pour over warm noodles.

Golden Noodle Casserole

½ lb. whole wheat or corn ribbons, vegetable noodles, or
   pasta shells
½ lb. firm tofu, cubed
3 leaves kale
1 small butternut squash
1 small onion
1 tsp. sesame oil
½ cup water
1 Tbsp. miso
⅔ tsp. tahini
pinch dried basil

Cook noodles, drain and rinse with cold water while noodles are still firm. Place in a bowl; add tofu. Wash kale, cut into thin strips, and add to noodles and tofu.

Cut squash in half, peel, and remove seeds. Cut into chunks and steam until soft. Slice onion; saute in oil until golden.

Place squash, onion, water, miso, tahini, and basil in blender; puree. Add to noodle mixture and toss. Bake in covered dish at 350°F for 20 minutes, then uncovered 5 more minutes.

Pumpkin Tofu Noodle Casserole
Very sweet and satisfying.

½ to 1 block tofu
½ medium sweet squash or pumpkin, cut in chunks
few drops shoyu
1 lb. whole wheat udon noodles
water
1 onion or leek, cut finely
2 tsp. vegetable oil
chopped parsley or scallions

Steam tofu 15 minutes, then mash. Cook squash with a small amount of water until soft, adding shoyu near the end of the cooking period. Mash squash and combine with tofu. Season with more shoyu, if needed.

Boil noodles in water until tender but not soggy. Drain noodles and put in a glass casserole dish.

Saute onion in oil until tender, then add to noodles and stir to coat them. Pour tofu and squash mixture over noodles and onions and place in a 350°F oven for 20 minutes. Garnish with chopped parsley or scallions and cover dish if casserole appears to be dry, then bake another 10 minutes. Serve with steamed greens.

Yakisoba

6 cups water
¼ tsp. sea salt
7 oz. soba
1 Tbsp. rice vinegar
1 tsp. toasted sesame oil
¼ cup freshly squeezed orange juice
1 Tbsp. miso
2 Tbsp. oil (or less)
1 small bunch parsley
½ small cabbage, cut into strips
½ medium onion, cut into rounds
¼ lb. broccoli, sliced
¼ cup carrots, slivered
2 Tbsp. water

Bring 6 cups water to a boil. Add salt and soba noodles. After water boils again, reduce heat to medium low and simmer 10 minutes or until noodles are tender. Drain and reserve noodles in 4 cups of warm water.

Combine vinegar, toasted sesame oil, orange juice, and miso in a small bowl. Set aside.

Add oil to a frying pan or wok. Heat to medium high. Add vegetables, 2 tablespoons water, and stir-fry for 5 minutes. Remove from heat.

Place drained noodles on individual plates. Arrange vegetables over noodles, and pour orange miso sauce on top. Serves 3.

Paul Motoyoshi

Herbed Walnut Yakisoba

Kobe Sauce:

1 Tbsp. light sesame, safflower, or olive oil
1 Tbsp. lemon juice
1 Tbsp. shoyu
1 Tbsp. rice syrup
1 tsp. miso
1 tsp. garlic, chopped
¾ tsp. rosemary
¼ tsp. ground black pepper

Combine ingredients; set aside.

This is a versatile and flavorful sauce that can also be used in stir-fry dishes, so you may wish to make a double or triple batch.

Herbed Walnuts:

¼ cup walnuts
½ tsp. chopped fresh parsley
½ tsp. chopped fresh basil, or ¼ tsp. dry basil
¼ tsp. sea salt
1 tsp. vegetable oil

Combine ingredients in a skillet over medium heat and stir with a wooden spoon for 3 to 4 minutes to coat walnuts with herbs and salt. When done, set aside.

Noodles:

- 7 oz. soba
- 6 cups water
- ¼ tsp. sea salt

Place noodles in boiling water and salt; simmer over medium-low heat for 12 minutes or until tender. Drain and reserve noodles in 4 cups of warm water.

Vegetable Topping:

- 2 Tbsp. oil (or less)
- ½ small cabbage, cut into strips
- ½ medium onion, cut into rings
- ¼ lb. broccoli, chopped
- ½ red pepper, cut into short strips
- 2 Tbsp. water

Add oil to wok or skillet and heat at medium setting. Add vegetables and stir-fry for 5 minutes; then remove from heat.

Combining Mixtures:

Place drained noodles on individual plates. Arrange sauteed vegetables over noodles. Drizzle kobe sauce over vegetables and sprinkle with herbed walnuts.

Paul Motoyoshi

Yakibowl (Yasai Donburi)

3 Tbsp. shoyu
1 Tbsp. rice syrup
1½ tsp. mirin (optional)
1 tsp. sesame seeds
1 tsp. sesame oil
½ tsp. miso
½ tsp. chopped garlic
1½ cups cooked brown rice, or cooked soba or udon
   noodles
2 tsp. safflower or toasted sesame oil
½ cup onion, sliced into rounds
¾ cup broccoli slices
½ cup cabbage slices
½ cup sprouts
1 Tbsp. water
½ lb. tofu, cut into ½-inch chunks

Combine shoyu, rice syrup, mirin, sesame seeds, sesame oil, miso, and garlic. Set aside.

Cook rice or noodles if not already on hand.

Add 1 teaspoon of oil to a frying pan or wok, and bring temperature to medium-high. Add onions, broccoli, cabbage, and sprouts. Mix these vegetables, then add water. Add tofu and cover pan with a lid and cook 3 minutes, stirring occasionally. Remove vegetables from pan.

To serve, place a few onion slices on the bottom of each bowl. Top with rice or noodles. Then arrange vegetables and tofu on top of this. Pour sesame sauce over each bowl. Serves 3.

Paul Motoyoshi

Paul's Pasta Primavera

Noodles:

6 to 8 cups water
¼ tsp. sea salt
16 ounces brown rice udon

Bring water to a boil. Add salt, then place noodles in boiling water. Bring water back to a boil, then reduce heat to medium-low and simmer 10 to 12 minutes. Drain and reserve noodles in 4 cups of warm water.

Broccoli Pesto Sauce:

2 cups water
3 cups broccoli, chopped
1 medium clove garlic, chopped
¼ cup water
½ tsp. basil
2 Tbsp. sunflower butter or chopped roasted walnuts
¼ tsp. sea salt

Bring 2 cups water to a boil. Add broccoli and garlic. Bring water to a boil again, then reduce heat to medium. Cook for 10 minutes. Drain and save the water.

Pour ¼ cup of the broccoli water into a blender. Add broccoli, basil, sunflower butter or walnuts, and salt. Blend for 30 seconds, stopping occasionally to stir pesto sauce by hand if necessary, until pesto sauce is somewhat smooth.

Sauteed Vegetables:

2 Tbsp. oil
¼ small cabbage, cut into strips
½ red pepper, cut into strips
¼ small cauliflower, cut into florets
pinch sea salt

Heat skillet at medium setting. Add oil, then add cabbage, pepper, cauliflower, and salt. Stir-fry lightly.

Combining Primavera:

Place noodles on individual serving plates. Arrange sauteed vegetables over pasta, and place dollop of broccoli pesto sauce over vegetables.

Paul Motoyoshi

Seitan

Seitan, a wheat product, has been used in China and Japan for centuries. Its meatlike appearance and chewy texture, along with its high protein content, make it a healthy addition to a vegetarian diet.

Seitan can be baked, boiled, marinated and broiled, pan-fried, stir-fried, deep-fried, added to soups and stews, or bar-bequed as shish kebabs. It can be found canned or in jars or airtight packages in many health food co-ops, macrobiotic stores, or mail-order catalogs. It tastes best, however, and is much less expensive when homemade. Once you learn the process, it goes very quickly and smoothly.

Seitan is made with wheat flour or gluten flour. Some people use only stoneground whole wheat flour, while others use a combination of whole wheat and white flour, and some use only gluten flour, which is a shorter method. I find the traditional method of using 100 percent whole wheat flour to be preferable and worth the extra effort. If you want to save time, make one very large batch or several bowls of seitan at a time, refrigerate some for immediate use, and freeze some.

To produce this concentrated protein source, a bread-like dough is kneaded and rinsed to remove the bran and starch. The resulting gluten balls must then be cooked, usually in a broth of kombu, water, shoyu, and ginger juice.

Cooked seitan can be stored with its cooking broth in jars in the refrigerator and then reheated or cooked in other dishes. It is best to use fresh seitan within 8 to 10 days. The cooking liquid can be added to a stew or thickened with kuzu root starch for a gravy. To freeze seitan, put several balls or meal-sized servings of cooked gluten in plastic bags.

Traditional Seitan Method

6 cups stoneground whole wheat bread flour or hard wheat
 flour
3 to 3½ cups cold water
1 to 2 cups additional whole wheat flour

Mix flour and water in a large bowl, adding additional flour
if necessary to make a stiff bread-like dough. Knead dough
in a bowl or on a floured board 10 to 12 minutes, then let
dough sit 20 minutes. Cover with cold water in a bowl and
let sit covered for several hours or overnight. (I usually let
dough sit for 1 to 3 hours.)

 Knead dough in water until it starts to break apart. Pour it
into a strainer, reserving liquid, then rinse seitan in fresh water. Use your hands to knead the seitan to rinse away the
bran and starch. (You may save the starch to use in breads,
puddings, sauces, or gravies.)

Wash the seitan as one large lump or break it into smaller balls and rinse and knead them individually. Either way, you will alternate warm and cold water and repeat the process of placing the dough in a bowl of water and squeezing and rinsing under warm then cold water, several times. It is "done" when no more white-milky water comes out of the seitan balls as you rinse and knead them. The texture will be stiff and stretchy, and you will not see brown bran bits as you stretch, pull, and rinse the dough in water.

Broth:

4 to 5 cups water
1/4 to 1/3 cup shoyu
4-inch piece kombu
ginger juice from large handful grated ginger (optional)

Bring water, shoyu, and kombu to a boil. Add seitan, either as one large lump or broken into bits and rolled into balls. When the seitan rises to the top of the water, add ginger juice. Continue to simmer the seitan for 3 to 4 hours or pressure cook 1 to 3 hours.

Pan-fried Seitan Steaks

Prepare seitan and stock as described in Traditional Seitan Method. Form seitan in 1 to 3 large pieces and cook in the stock. Cut the cooked seitan in ¼-inch steak cutlets and roll in corn flour or arrowroot powder to coat.

Lightly coat a cast iron skillet with sesame oil. Heat the oil until it begins to sizzle, then add the floured seitan cutlets and cook over medium-high heat until one side is very well browned and lightly charred. Then turn it over and cook the other side. This lightly charred color and taste will make it very much like steak or veal cutlets. Cook each side again to make it crispier, if desired.

Herbed Seitan Saute

Looks like meat; tastes rich and hearty. It is high in protein and easily digested.

1 large white onion, minced or cut in fine crescents
1 tsp. to 1 Tbsp. oil (olive, safflower, or light sesame)
3 cups minced seitan
¼ to ½ tsp. dried oregano
¼ to ½ tsp. dried dill weed
2 cups liquid from seitan or 1¾ cup water plus 1 to 2 tsp.
   shoyu
2 cups fresh mushrooms
1 Tbsp. sesame tahini (optional)

Saute onions in oil over medium-high heat until golden. Add seitan pieces and stir well. Add herbs and 1 cup of the liquid, continuing to stir over medium to high heat. Add mushrooms. When liquid is absorbed (2 to 3 minutes), add the rest of the liquid and tahini, and continue to stir to thicken and until almost all of the liquid is absorbed. Serves 4 to 6 people as a side dish.

Serving Suggestions:

– Serve with Onion Soup or Daikon, Onion, and Wakame Miso Soup, brown rice, steamed broccoli, baked squash or boiled sweet squash, kale with sauerkraut or other pickles.

Seitan Stir-fry

1 or 2 medium-sized onions, chopped
12 to 15 mushrooms, chopped
1 medium carrot, cut in matchsticks
pinch sea salt
1 cup seitan, cooked in broth in small pieces
1 bunch broccoli, chopped
$\frac{1}{4}$ cup purple cabbage, cut in thin strips
water
shoyu (optional)
mirin (optional)

Saute onion until golden. Add mushrooms, carrots and a pinch of salt. Saute and stir until fragrant. Stir in seitan and cook 2 to 3 minutes. Add broccoli, cabbage and a small amount of water as needed to prevent burning. Cook until broccoli is tender. Add shoyu and mirin as desired.

Seitan Stew

2 onions, cut in large crescents
2 turnips
3 carrots
2 rutabagas
2 to 3 cups seitan, cooked, cut in 1-inch cubes
water
1 Tbsp. shoyu or to taste
1½ Tbsp. kuzu dissolved in 3 Tbsp. water (optional)
2 tsp. juice from grated fresh ginger root

Wash and cut root vegetables in wedges. Layer vegetables in a pot and top with chunks of seitan. Add water to a depth of ½ inch. Bring to a boil and cook for 20 to 30 minutes or until vegetables are tender. Add a dash of shoyu for flavor and kuzu to thicken if necessary. Add ginger juice last.

Serving suggestions:

– Serve with steamed greens and a brown rice combination such as Wheat Berry Rice or Barley with Rice, or rice with seeds or nuts such as Rice with Sunnies or Rice with Walnuts or Roasted Pumpkin Seeds.

Seitan Sandwich

This resembles a roast beef sandwich — it's a quick and easy sandwich to make and has a distinct taste of its own.

    seitan, cooked in stock
    2 slices whole wheat bread, sourdough bread, or bun per
       sandwich
    stoneground mustard
    naturally-aged sauerkraut or dill pickle slices
    steamed kale or raw lettuce
    tomatoes
    sliced red onions and/or sprouts

Slice seitan very thin and allow several slices for each sandwich. Make sandwiches from seitan slices and other ingredients as desired. Serve open faced or covered; hot, cold, or at room temperature.

Serving Suggestions:

– Serve with baked parsnips or baked potato chips, boiled corn-on-the-cob or Blanched Salad.

Breads And Pastries

Sourdough Raisin Bread

- 8 cups whole wheat flour
- 3 cups cooked rice
- 2 to 3 Tbsp. miso
- 2 to 3 Tbsp. barley malt syrup
- approximately 4 cups warm water
- 2 cups raisins

Mix all ingredients and knead approximately 300 times. Let mixture rise about 24 hours in a warm, damp place. Lightly oil two bread pans, form loaves and place loaves in pans. Let rise. Bake at 350°F for about 40 minutes. Brush with corn oil while baking or before putting loaves in the oven, if desired.

Lemon Corn Muffins

A pleasantly sour bread

3 to 4 cups cooked grain (leftover rice, barley, whole oat
   porridge, or quinoa work well)
4 to 5 cups warm water or liquid from cooking noodles
3 to 4 cups corn flour, approximately
1 cup whole wheat flour
¼ to ½ tsp. sea salt
⅓ cup corn oil
¼ to ⅓ cup rice syrup
1 tsp. vanilla
4 Tbsp. ground flaxseed
¾ cup boiling water
grated rind of ½ lemon
1½ tsp. baking soda

Leave grain at cool room temperature for several days. Cover cooked and soured grain with water and let it sit at room temperature overnight or longer (12 to 24 hours). Add 3 cups corn flour, whole wheat flour, and salt; let this mixture sit 6 to 8 hours. Batter should be runny.

Preheat oven to 400°F. Heat corn oil and rice syrup until it boils. Remove from heat, add vanilla, and add to batter.

Grind flaxseed in a coffee mill or blender; pour boiling water over flaxseed meal and let it sit 15 minutes. Mix or whip until fluffy, then add to batter.

Add lemon peel, baking soda, and additional corn flour to make a thick batter. Spoon into lightly oiled muffin pans, filling each cup ¾ full. Bake for 15 to 20 minutes or until golden on top. Serve with rice syrup or apple butter. Makes 16 to 20 muffins.

Wheat-free Pancakes

1 Tbsp. flaxseed meal
3 Tbsp. boiling water
½ cup white or brown rice flour
⅔ cup barley flour
⅓ cup rolled oats
½ cup pulverized rolled oats or oat flour
¼ tsp. sea salt
½ tsp. baking soda
1 tsp. baking powder
1 to 1½ cups soy milk or amasake and water
1 Tbsp. maple syrup or 2 Tbsp. rice syrup (omit sweetener if
    using amasake)
1 tsp. cinnamon (optional)

Mix flaxseed meal and water. Let sit 15 minutes and whip
with a fork. Blend dry ingredients and wet ingredients separately, then mix together. Lightly oil and heat a cast iron
skillet or pancake griddle. Pour ⅛ to ¼ cup batter per pancake on the griddle. When the cakes bubble, flip them and
cook the other side approximately 2 to 3 minutes. Arrange
on a wire rack to cool or on a plate. Serve warm or refrigerate them for quick meals later.

Pancake Mix Pancakes

There are a number of good natural whole grain pancake
mixes at your local co-op, natural foods store, or the health
food section of your local grocery store. These include buckwheat, wheat-free corn, multigrain, wheat and soy, and other pancake mixes.

Look for one that contains no sugar, honey, dextrose, corn syrup, eggs, buttermilk, or artificial ingredients. A good mix should contain several kinds of flour, perhaps sea salt, and baking soda or baking powder.

Tips:

– Substitute soy milk (plain or vanilla) for milk.

– Either omit the eggs completely and use soy milk to make up for the difference, or use a flaxseed binder to replace the eggs: Grind 2 Tbsp. flaxseed in a coffee/spice mill or other food grinder. Pour 6 tablespoons boiling water over the flaxseed meal, then let it sit 15 minutes. Whisk with a fork. This amount replaces 2 eggs.

– The batter should be runny so add more liquid as needed to make a light pancake. Experiment with the first few pancakes.

– For each pancake, pour ¼ cup of batter on a heated, oiled cast iron skillet, griddle, or stainless steel skillet. When pancake bubbles, flip it over. Repeat until batter is used up.

– Serve with applesauce, amasake squash puree, raisin syrup, rice malt kuzu, or natural fruit-sweetened preserves.

– Extra pancakes store well in the refrigerator in a covered bowl or in an airtight plastic bag. They make great leftovers for a quick breakfast. Just steam or warm them in a toaster oven or regular oven.

Jan's Whole Wheat Pie Crust

The best recipe I've ever found for crust. Great for turnovers, pies, etc.

⅔ cup boiling water
¼ cup sesame oil
2 cups whole wheat pastry flour
½ tsp. sea salt

Beat water and oil until white, preferably in a blender. Mix with flour and salt, then knead 1 to 2 minutes. Refrigerate 30 minutes. Roll out on floured board. Fit into pie pan and crimp edges. Bake 15 minutes at 400°F.

To prevent burning or a tough crust, place a pan of water on the lower rack of the oven. Makes 1 crust for a 9-inch pie.

For fruit pies:

Roll out crust, fit into pie pan and fill with stewed fruit; bake 15 to 20 minutes at 350° to 375°F.

For Turnovers:

Roll out dough, cut in 3-inch to 5-inch circles, place filling on one side, fold dough over, and pinch edges together. Bake on lightly oiled cookie sheets at 350° to 375°F for 15 to 20 minutes or until golden.

Fill with:
- Sauteed tofu and vegetables;
- Cooked beans with vegetables;
- Sauteed seitan, onion, mushrooms;
- Curried vegetables with potato;
- Sauteed tempeh and vegetables;

- Chopped apples, cinnamon, raisins, tossed with
  barley malt or rice syrup and lemon;
- Soaked dried fruit or cooked stewed fruit.

Whole Wheat Crust

2 cups whole wheat pastry flour
pinch sea salt
2 Tbsp. corn or sesame oil
½ cup ice water

Mix flour and salt. Add oil and mix thoroughly with fingers
until there are no lumps. Add water and mix to make a
dough. Do not overhandle dough or it will become tough.
Roll as thin as possible on a floured board. Line pie pan and
crimp edge. Bake at 400°F for 15 minutes. Makes 1 crust for a
9-inch pie.

Jan Badillo-Cochran

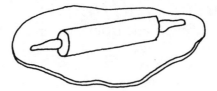

Sourdough Whole Wheat Crust

1 cup cooked rice or other grain
4 cups water
4 to 6 cups freshly ground whole wheat flour
pinch sea salt

Three days ahead of time, cover rice or other grain with water. Cover with cheesecloth and let sit at room temperature for 3 days.

Combine the sour liquid with whole wheat flour and salt to make a stiff dough. Knead 10 to 15 minutes. Place in an oiled bowl and let it rise all day or night in a warm place.

Press into pizza pan and top with sauce and desired toppings, or use for vegetable pie. Bake at 325° to 350°F for 20 to 30 minutes.

Jan Badillo-Cochran

Essene Bread Stuffing
A wheat-free stuffing made from sprouted grains

3 garlic cloves, minced
3 Tbsp. olive oil or light sesame oil
1⅔ cups chopped onion
2 cups chopped celery
5 cups sprouted essene bread, crumbled (rye, millet-rice, or seed bread), or other whole grain bread
1 cup chopped walnuts or sunflower seeds, toasted (optional)
1 cup water
¼ tsp. sea salt
⅔ cup chopped fresh parsley

Saute garlic in oil 2 minutes; add onions, stir, and saute 2 minutes. Add celery, stir, and saute 1 to 2 minutes. Add essene bread and stir. Add chopped walnuts or sunflower seeds, ½ cup of the water, and salt. Stir well to prevent bottom from sticking or burning. Add parsley and the remaining water and continue to stir 3 minutes or until well mixed. Turn off and set aside.

Serving Suggestions:

– Stuff a tofu "turkey" or a seitan "roast."

– Serve as a side dish to steamed vegetables, baked or broiled tofu or tempeh cutlets, squash soup or puree, and brown rice.

Low-fat Tortilla Chips

≡ 1 package (12) whole corn tortillas
≡ corn oil or toasted sesame oil

Cut tortillas into quarters and brush lightly with oil. Place on baking tray and bake at 300°F for 10 to 15 minutes. Turn chips for even baking, if necessary.

Sauces and Condiments

Sauces and Gravies

Chestnut Puree
Very sweet and creamy.

2 cups dry chestnuts
6 cups water
2 pinches sea salt

Soak chestnuts in 6 cups water overnight. Pressure cook 1 hour. Add salt and simmer 30 minutes. Let cool and puree in blender. It will thicken naturally.
   Save extra puree in a jar in the refrigerator.

Serving Suggestions:
– Pour or spoon over:
- baked squash;
- baked onion;
- baked mochi puffs;
- baked apples;
- soft cooked Brussels sprouts;
- pancakes or waffles, with a dollop of apple butter;
- nishime-cooked carrots.

Onion Gravy

1 onion, sliced in crescents
1 to 2 tsp. toasted sesame oil
1½ cups water, soup stock, or twig tea
2 Tbsp. kuzu
2 to 2½ Tbsp. shoyu or miso
¼ tsp. juice from grated fresh ginger root

Saute onions in sesame oil until translucent. Add 1 cup water or stock and simmer. Mix kuzu with ½ cup of the liquid; add to onions. Add shoyu, then ginger juice. Simmer for 2 minutes or until mixture thickens and becomes clear.

Variation:

– Saute 3 or 4 soaked and sliced shiitake mushrooms with onions. Use ½ to 1 teaspoon minced or pressed garlic in place of ginger juice.

Creamy Pumpkin and Oats Puree

1 kabocha or Hokkaido pumpkin, cubed (8 to 10 cups)
water
1 large onion, chopped
several pinches sea salt
⅓ cup rolled oats
3 to 4 cups water

Pressure cook squash with a small amount of water for 15 to 20 minutes. Saute onion with a small amount of water until translucent; add to pumpkin and puree in blender or by hand. Add salt to taste.

Cook oats in water for 5 to 6 minutes; add to puree. Bring mixture to boil and simmer, covered, over lowest heat for 1 to 3 hours.

Variations:

– Use carrots, squash, and onion.

– Use rutabaga, carrot, and onion.

– Use parsnip, squash, and onion.

– Use pumpkin, celery, and onion.

– Add chickpea miso to the puree.

– Garnish with ao-nori flakes or crumbled nori.

– Make a creamy, thick pudding by omitting the oats, or a porridge by increasing the oats.

Non-Dairy "Cheese" Sauce

⅓ cup kuzu
2 cups water
⅓ cup raw sesame tahini
1½ to 2 Tbsp. chickpea miso
1 Tbsp. finely grated carrot

Dissolve kuzu in 1 cup of water. Mix in tahini, miso, and carrot; blend until smooth. Add remaining water. Heat mixture in saucepan and stir constantly until it becomes thick. Pour over vegetables (it's great over cauliflower and broccoli), noodles, or rice. Can also be baked, if desired.

Variations:

– Add pureed tofu, grated mochi, or minced onions.

Sesame Sauce with Thyme

⅔ cup sesame butter or tahini
1 cup cool water
2 Tbsp. shoyu
2 tsp. ground dried thyme

Place all ingredients in a small saucepan and bring to a boil. Simmer and stir for 2 to 3 minutes or until oil and water are mixed. Sauce will thicken as it cools. Store extra sauce in a jar in the refrigerator; reheat and dilute if desired.

Serving Suggestions:

- Serve over grains and vegetables. Especially good with steamed greens or carrots.

- This is great over pasta – whole wheat udon noodles, spinach noodles, or soba. Lightly coat warm noodles with sauce or rinse noodles after cooking, place on plates, top with steamed vegetables, and add sauce.

Sunflower Basil Sauce

¾ cup sunflower butter
1 cup water
1 tsp. crushed dried basil or thyme
2 to 3 Tbsp. shoyu

Bring all ingredients to a boil in a saucepan. Simmer 3 minutes, stirring well. Turn off heat and stir well until completely mixed and thickened.

Serving suggestions:

- Serve over noodles or steamed vegetables.

- Refrigerate extra sauce. It can be served without reheating.

Umeboshi Tofu Sauce

¼ cup umeboshi vinegar
1 cup water
1 lb. soft tofu

Mix vinegar and water; add tofu. Poach in marinade 10 to 15 minutes, then puree with liquid until creamy. Pour over steamed cauliflower and carrot or leeks, or use as a noodle and vegetable sauce or topping.

Tofu Sauce

1 lb. tofu
2 to 2½ Tbsp. barley miso or rice miso
2 to 3 Tbsp. tahini
2 Tbsp. brown rice vinegar or lemon juice
2 cloves garlic, minced or pressed
umeboshi paste (optional)
1 to 2 Tbsp. vegetable oil
up to ⅓ cup water
⅓ cup minced scallion
1 large handful fresh parsley, minced
ao-nori flakes (optional)

Steam tofu 15 minutes and crumble into blender pitcher. Add miso, tahini, vinegar or lemon juice, garlic, umeboshi paste, and oil. Blenderize, adding a few spoonfuls of water at a time to make a smooth consistency. Add scallions, parsley, and garlic; stir with a wooden spoon to blend mixture. Add more water as needed to make a thick, creamy sauce that resembles sour cream. Garnish with ao-nori flakes, if desired.

Tofu Guacamole

8 oz. tofu, sliced or cubed
2 large or 3 medium avocados, soft and ripe
3 cloves garlic, grated or pressed
juice of ½ lemon, or to taste
3 Tbsp. umeboshi vinegar
2 to 3 Tbsp. grated fresh onion

Steam tofu 5 to 10 minutes, then cool. Blenderize tofu or mash well. Add peeled and pitted avocados, garlic, lemon juice, vinegar, and onion. Mix with a fork. Adjust seasonings to taste. Cover tightly and chill, or serve immediately. It's best if made just before serving. Serves 6 to 10.

Serving Suggestions:

– Serve with baked beans, stoneground corn chips or tortillas, brown rice, steamed or blanched vegetables, rice cakes and sprouts or greens.

Tofu Sour Cream

1 lb. soft tofu, sliced
2 to 4 Tbsp. olive oil or light sesame oil
½ cup water
½ tsp. sea salt
juice of ⅓ lemon
2 to 3 cloves garlic, minced or pressed
¼ to ⅓ cup fresh minced parsley or 3 minced scallions
½ to 1 cup chopped, rinsed black olives (optional)
walnut pieces, chopped and roasted (optional)
¼ to ½ cup capers (optional)

Steam tofu 10 to 12 minutes and let cool. Blenderize tofu
with oil, water, salt, lemon juice, garlic, and parsley or scallions. Taste and adjust seasonings if desired, or stir in olives,
walnut pieces, or capers.

Walnut Miso Gravy

2 cups walnuts
4 Tbsp. barley miso or other dark miso
6 cups cold water or kombu stock
3 Tbsp. kuzu or 4 Tbsp. arrowroot powder

Rinse walnuts in a sieve. Place on baking sheet and roast at

250°F for 10 to 12 minutes or until slightly golden and nutty smelling. Chop coarsely with knife.

Mix miso with water or stock; dissolve kuzu or arrowroot powder in this liquid. Pour in saucepan and cook at medium heat until mixture begins to thicken. Taste to see that flavor is strong but not salty. Add more miso if desired.

Add walnut pieces and reduce heat to low. Simmer for 15 to 20 minutes. Add more water if sauce is too thick.

Serving suggestions:

– Serve poured over Millet Mound.

– Save leftover gravy in a jar or glass bowl. Sauce thickens when chilled so more water may be added when reheating. Leftover gravy is good mixed with leftover rice, celery, carrot and minced onions to make burgers or mixed with lentils and baked.

Dressings

Green Goddess

2 cups roasted pumpkin seeds, ground
2 cups fresh parsley, chopped
2 cups water
1 umeboshi plum
¼ cup pickle juice or sauerkraut juice
1½ Tbsp. white miso

Blenderize ingredients until creamy. Serve over salads or steamed vegetables.

Lime Vinaigrette

¼ to ½ cup fresh lime juice
⅓ to ⅔ cup olive oil
⅓ cup rice vinegar or cider vinegar
1 to 3 cloves garlic, minced or pressed
3 Tbsp. umeboshi vinegar (optional)
¼ to ½ tsp. sea salt
3 Tbsp. warm water
½ to 1 tsp. dried basil
½ to 1 tsp. dried dill weed

Place all ingredients in a bottle, cover, and shake well. Chill and store in refrigerator. Serve with raw or blanched salads.

Mustard and Mayo Sauce

½ cup soy mayonnaise
1 tsp. stoneground mustard
¼ cup water
½ to 1 tsp. shoyu (to taste)

Blend ingredients until smooth.

Serving Suggestions:
– Serve over:
- Seitan cutlets with fresh steamed kale or broccoli and rice or noodles;
- Boiled tempeh with steamed greens and rice;
- Pan-fried seitan cutlets with kale, carrots, and rice.

Miso Nut Butter Dressing

1 cup peanut butter or sesame butter
1 Tbsp. barley miso or sweet rice miso
2 to 3 Tbsp. rice syrup
1 Tbsp. rice vinegar or lemon juice

Mix all ingredients, adding water to blend for desired consistency. Store in a jar in the refrigerator and use as needed.

Pour over steamed or blanched vegetables, rice and bean loaves, noodles, grain and vegetable salads, soy burgers, or tofu cutlets.

Herbed Pumpkin Seed Dressing

1 cup green pumpkin seeds
2 Tbsp. brown rice vinegar
2 Tbsp. herb vinegar or lemon juice with ½ tsp. each basil,
    dill, and/or oregano
¾ to 1 cup water
1 Tbsp. miso

Roast seeds in a dry cast iron skillet, stirring well. When they
are golden and aromatic, grind them in a nut and seed
grinder, spice mill, or coffee mill.

Mix vinegars and dissolve miso in water. Mash to break
up lumps. Mix all ingredients well.

Serve on blanched vegetable salads with brown rice.

Seed Dressing

1 cup pumpkin seeds
⅔ cup sunflower seeds
1 cup water
1 Tbsp. rice vinegar or juice from natural pickles
1 Tbsp. umeboshi vinegar

Roast pumpkin seeds and sunflower seeds separately in a
dry skillet. Grind in a blender or nut mill. Blend all ingredients or mix well.

Variations:

– Omit sunflower seeds and umeboshi vinegar and use
   1⅔ cups pumpkin seeds and 1 to 2 tablespoons umeboshi
   paste.

– Omit sunflower seeds and umeboshi vinegar and use ⅔ cup sesame seeds and 1 to 2 tablespoons umeboshi paste.

– Omit pumpkin seeds and vinegars and use 1 cup sunflower seeds, ½ cup sauerkraut juice, and 1 tsp. umeboshi paste.

– Omit sunflower seeds and add chopped parsley or scallions and ⅛ to ¼ cup ao-nori flakes.

Tangy Sun Seed Dressing

1¾ cups sunflower seeds
1½ tsp. lemon juice
1 Tbsp. brown rice vinegar
2 Tbsp. umeboshi vinegar
1 cup water

Dry-roast sunflower seeds in a cast iron skillet for 6 to 10 minutes or until golden. Stir well to prevent burning. If you prefer, bake them on a cookie sheet at 200°F for 6 to 10 minutes; do not burn. Grind seeds in a nut grinder, spice mill, or coffee mill. Mix sunflower seed meal with other ingredients.

Variations and Serving suggestions:

– Use 1½ tablespoon lemon juice for a tangier dressing.

– Toss with blanched vegetable salad.

– Serve at the table to accompany rice or noodles and assorted vegetables.

Sesame Mustard

¼ cup sesame seeds
⅓ cup mustard seeds
1 umeboshi plum
1 Tbsp. barley miso or rice miso
2 to 3 tsp. brown rice vinegar
¼ cup water
1 to 2 tsp. shoyu

Toast sesame seeds in cast iron skillet until they pop, turn golden, and smell nutty, approximately 8 to 10 minutes. Roast mustard seeds until they brown and smell very pungent. Grind each in a suribachi or spice mill. Blend with remaining ingredients and mix well. Place in jars and refrigerate. Best if used within 2 to 3 weeks.

Serving Suggestions:

– Spread on toast and make a sandwich with sauerkraut and steamed kale.

– Serve with pan-fried tempeh, onions, and sauerkraut on bread or with brown rice.

Spreads

Almond Pate

1 cup roasted almonds, chopped finely
1 cup bread crumbs
1 medium onion, chopped
3 to 4 stalks celery, chopped
1 Tbsp. sesame oil or corn oil, or water
½ tsp. dill
½ tsp. thyme
1 clove garlic, crushed (optional)
1 tsp. shoyu
1 to 3 tsp. pickle juice
chopped parsley

Combine almonds with bread crumbs. Saute onions and celery in oil or water. When transparent, add dill, thyme, and garlic. Combine with almonds and bread crumbs and add shoyu and enough pickle juice to hold the mixture together. Form into a large ball, and roll in chopped parsley. Refrigerate until ready to serve.

Mim Collins-Drewry

Chickpea Vegetable Spread

1 small onion, finely chopped (optional)
1 small carrot, finely chopped (optional)
5 Brussels sprouts, finely chopped (optional)
1 cup cooked chickpeas, mashed
shoyu or miso to taste
kuzu dissolved in cold water (optional)

Place vegetables, as desired, in a pot with chickpeas on top.
Add a small amount of water to prevent burning. Cook over
medium heat for about 30 minutes or until vegetables are
soft. Add shoyu or miso to taste and thicken with kuzu if
necessary. Puree if desired.

Chickpea Spread

1 small onion
1 clove garlic, minced (optional)
1 cup cooked chickpeas
1 to 2 Tbsp. tahini
1 Tbsp. gomashio
 shoyu or light miso to taste

Saute onion and garlic in a lightly oiled skillet. Puree chickpeas in a food mill or suribachi. Add tahini softened in a little cool water. Add gomashio and sauteed onion. Mix well,
adding shoyu or miso to taste.

Pate de la Mer

- 2 cups dry hijiki (or 1 cup hijiki and 1 cup arame)
- 1 medium onion, sliced (optional)
- ¼ cup mirin (optional)
- ¼ cup shoyu
- 2 to 3 Tbsp. stoneground mustard

Rinse and soak sea vegetables about 10 minutes; reserve soak water. If using onion, saute in a little sesame oil in a 1-quart pan. Add sea vegetables, mirin, shoyu, soak water, and additional water if necessary to cover them.

Simmer over low heat until hijiki is completely cooked, about 1 hour. If any liquid remains, remove lid and let it cook off. Stir in mustard. Blend the whole mixture in a food processor or blender to make a paste. Serve with assorted crackers.

Variations and Serving Suggestions:

– Try using miso instead of shoyu.

– Place pate on small rice crackers and mini rice cakes, and decorate with flower-shaped carrot, cucumber, and tofu slices which have been cut with tiny cookie cutters.

– Garnish with minced scallions, parsley, roasted chopped walnuts, or sesame seeds.

John Snyder

Jan's Savory Miso Sunflower Spread

1 lb. tofu
½ cup sunflower seeds, roasted
2 Tbsp. lemon juice or vinegar
2 Tbsp. rice malt
3 Tbsp. minced onion
3 Tbsp. red or white miso
1 Tbsp. tahini
⅛ to ¼ cup water

Steam tofu 10 minutes. Add to blender with remaining ingredients and blend. Add water to achieve desired consistency.

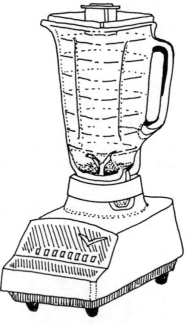

Condiments

Gomashio

Gomashio is used as a condiment at the table. It can be used
as salt, although more liberally. It contains zinc, calcium,
magnesium, and other minerals. Sprinkle gomashio with a
spoon on grains and vegetable dishes.

≡ 1 Tbsp. sea salt
≡ 1 cup sesame seeds

Lightly roast salt in a dry skillet and grind to powder in a suribachi. Set aside. Rinse seeds in a special sesame seed wash-
er or a very fine mesh strainer. Place in a hot, dry skillet and
stir with a wooden spoon until dry. Reduce heat if necessary
to prevent burning. Continue stirring and watch seeds so
they don't pop out of the pan. Roast until they are golden
brown and pop. (Black sesame seeds are trickier, so go slow-
er.)

To test for doneness, place a seed on your ring finger and
press in the middle of the seed with your thumb. The seeds
are done when they pop open and oil comes out. They will
be very aromatic and smell oily and nutty. Taste a few — bitter seeds are burned or underdone.

Grind seeds in the suribachi with lightly roasted and
ground sea salt until 60 percent of the seeds are finely
ground.

Sesame Seaweed Powder

≡   1 part seaweed, choose 1 kind
≡   4 to 8 parts sesame seeds, roasted and ground

Roast seaweed in oven at 250°F as follows:

≡   nori, 1 to 2 minutes
≡   wakame, 5 to 10 minutes
≡   dulse, 6 to 8 minutes
≡   kombu, 15 to 20 minutes

Seaweed should be crisp. Crumble between your hands or grind in a suribachi or mortar and pestle. Mix with sesame seed and sprinkle on vegetables, rice, or noodles.

Variations:

– Use ground Roasted Pumpkin Seeds in place of sesame seeds.

– Omit seeds and use seaweed powder alone.

Toasted Wakame Powder

Roast wakame on a cookie sheet in the oven at 200° to 250° for about 10 minutes, or until crispy but not burned. Crumble in a suribachi or by hand. Store in a jar and use instead of salt to season vegetables, rice, or noodles.

Shoyu Roasted Almonds

Preheat oven to 250° to 300°F.

Rinse raw almonds in a sieve under running water and spread on a baking sheet. Bake until golden and aromatic, but do not overroast. Stir every 5 to 8 minutes to prevent burning and uneven cooking. Almonds will be done after 10 to 20 minutes, depending on oven.

When nuts are almost done, sprinkle them with a mixture of 1 teaspoon each shoyu and water per 2 cups almonds, if desired. Roast 2 to 3 minutes until liquid has evaporated.

Store in a glass jar and use for snacks or to chop and sprinkle over cooked grain or steamed vegetables. Refrigerate them after a week.

Mixed Seed Seasoning

⅓ cup sesame seeds
⅓ cup pumpkin seeds
⅓ cup sunflower seeds
1 Tbsp. sea salt

Dry-roast seeds separately until seeds are golden brown and nutty smelling. Roast salt in dry skillet for 2 to 3 minutes, stirring frequently. Grind seeds and salt in a small nut and seed mill or suribachi.

Store in a jar or ceramic pot and serve at the table on hot cereals, rice, noodles, and/or vegetables.

This combination yields a complete protein and balance of zinc, potassium, iron, magnesium, calcium, and several other minerals.

Roasted Pumpkin Seeds

Rinse 3 cups raw, green, hulled pumpkin seeds. Drain and place in a hot, dry, cast iron or stainless steel pot or skillet. Stir with a wooden spoon until the seeds are dry, then turn heat to medium. When seeds start to pop, turn heat to medium-low. Keep stirring gently 5 to 8 minutes, or until seeds puff up and some pop open.

For seasoned pumpkin seeds, remove pot or skillet from heat and sprinkle seeds with a mixture of 1 teaspoon each water and umeboshi vinegar or shoyu. Return to stove and heat seeds 1 or 2 minutes or until liquid dries.

Store seeds in a jar or bowl in your refrigerator.

Plain roasted pumpkin seeds are good with cooked arame or hijiki seaweed. They can be ground in a suribachi, mini coffee grinder or nut and seed mill to make dressings for cooked vegetables and grains.

Seasoned seeds are great as a snack or served on vegetables or rice.

Roasted Squash Seeds

If you cook a lot of winter squash, you'll find yourself scooping lots of seeds from the centers of these vegetables. They can be roasted rather than discarded.

Rinse pulp and seeds in a sieve to remove pulp. Spread seeds on a baking sheet and place in a 275° to 300°F oven. Every 10 minutes, gently stir with a spoon so they roast evenly. After 20 or 30 minutes they should be dry and begin to turn a light golden color and puff up. Sprinkle a dash of shoyu over seeds, stirring while you sprinkle. Bake 5 to 10 more minutes.

Taste to make sure they do not become overroasted. The seeds will bake a bit more after you remove them from the oven, so be alert. Allow seeds to cool, then store in a glass jar or ceramic dish.

Serving suggestions:

– Sprinkle over brown rice or other cooked grain.

– Toss in marinated or plain vegetable salads.

– Serve as snacks.

Pickles

Quick Sweet-Sour Cabbage

½ head white cabbage, cut finely in strips
2 Tbsp. water
1 Tbsp. umeboshi vinegar
1 Tbsp. brown rice vinegar
2 to 3 Tbsp. poppy seeds

Heat skillet over high heat; add cabbage, water, and vinegars. Cook and stir gently with chopsticks for 2 to 3 minutes. Reduce heat and simmer 20 to 30 minutes. Cabbage will get darker and shrink.

Roast poppy seeds in dry skillet for 2 to 3 minutes. Sprinkle over cabbage and serve.

Miso Garlic Pickles

☰ organically grown garlic
☰ buckwheat miso or hatcho miso

Prepare jar or ceramic crock by sterilizing with boiling water. Peel garlic cloves but do not cut or mince. Place a layer of miso in the bottom of the jar or crock. Place a layer of garlic over miso, cover garlic with miso, and repeat until jar is full to within ½ inch from the top.

Cover and set in a cool, dry place. You can remove garlic anytime after 3 months and use as needed, then put the jar back in a cool, dry place in your cupboard or refrigerator. Miso garlic pickles can be aged for 2 years. The garlic actually becomes less garlicky as the miso takes on the garlic essence.

Serving Suggestions:

– Use the garlic as a pickle or condiment at the end of a meal to aid digestion. Allow 2 to 3 cloves per person.

– Chop the garlic and mix with salads or beans.

– Use the miso to season hummus (chickpea spread), tofu dips, lentil pate, casseroles, and sauces.

Pickled Pink Radishes

≡ 1 bunch red radishes
≡ ½ to ⅔ cup apple cider vinegar or equal parts ume vinegar
    and rice vinegar

Rinse radishes and scrub to remove any dirt. Cut them into
very thin rounds. Place in bowl or glass dish and pour vinegar over them. Let sit 2 to 5 hours, occasionally turning radish pieces to make sure they all turn pink and become pickled.

When ready to serve, remove pickles from liquid. Reserve liquid to use in salad dressings. Serve 3 to 4 slices radish pickles for each person. They look especially nice next to
arame with sesame seeds, steamed kale, cheesy baked tofu
or tempeh, carrots or squash, nishime-style or pureed.

Umeboshi Plums

Umeboshi plums, which are available at many health food
stores and co-ops, can be used inside rice balls or nori-maki
sushi, or mashed and used in sauces or dressings. Half an
umeboshi plum is sometimes placed under the tongue to
ease a headache or upset stomach.

Umeboshi vinegar is the liquid from naturally aged umeboshi red plums. It can be sprinkled on steamed vegetables
and salads. It is very concentrated and salty and may be diluted with an equal amount of water.

There is also a special drink one can make with kuzu root,
umeboshi plum and water:

1 heaping tsp. kuzu root powder
1 cup water
1 tsp. shoyu
½ to 1 umeboshi plum, without pit
⅛ tsp. grated fresh ginger (optional)

Dissolve kuzu in water and bring to a boil. Simmer, stirring constantly until it becomes transparent. Stir in shoyu, umeboshi plum, and ginger. Drink while it is hot.

Wakame Cucumber Pickle Relish

1 scant cup dry wakame
1.75-oz. or 50-gram package sushi cucumber pickles
1 to 1½ Tbsp. stoneground mustard
2 to 3 Tbsp. natural sauerkraut

Soak wakame in water to cover for 15 minutes, then boil 10 minutes with lid off to evaporate most of the liquid. Let it cool, then cut finely.

Dice cucumber pickle; add to wakame. Add mustard and sauerkraut; mix and serve as a condiment. Makes 8 to 10 servings.

Shoyu Mushrooms

6 cups fresh mushrooms, rinsed, cut in slices
⅔ cup shoyu
1½ cups water

Combine ingredients. Cook in a large pot with lid ajar for 1 hour or until liquid is absorbed.

Serving Suggestions:

– Use as a pickle-like condiment over rice, 1 teaspoon per person.

– Add to steamed broccoli.

– Lightly saute 1 bunch collard greens, cut finely, in a pan brushed with toasted sesame oil. Add 2 teaspoons water and cook 3 to 4 minutes. Mix in ½ or more cups shoyu mushrooms.

– Serve with delicatta squash, barley and rice, arame seaweed, and broccoli or kale.

– Serve with Millet Mound and Walnut Miso Gravy, split pea miso soup with wakame, carrot rutabaga puree or cooked squash, and fresh greens.

Beverages

Apple Zinger

≡ 3 cups water
1 teabag red zinger or similar herb tea
3 cups apple juice

Boil water. Add tea bag and let tea steep in a teapot or covered saucepan with the heat off for approximately 5 minutes. Mix tea with apple juice. Serve with a lemon wedge. Serves 3 to 4.

Variation:

– Chill zinger or let it cool at room temperature. Serve as a summer punch with lemon wedges squeezed into the tea.

Bancha Tea

Bancha tea is available as loose tea or in tea bags. Sometimes it is called roasted kukicha twig tea. You will want the roasted twigs and not the green tea.

≡ 1½ to 3 Tbsp. roasted twigs
6 cups water

Bring water and twigs to a boil and simmer 5 to 10 minutes. Strain and serve. You can reuse twigs for several pots of tea.

Bancha Tea with Lemon

1 bancha tea bag
3 cups water
lemon

Bring to a boil, reduce heat, and simmer 3 to 4 minutes. Turn off heat and let it steep, covered, 5 to 6 minutes. Serve with a squeeze of fresh lemon. Serves 3.

Bancha Tea with Apple Juice

Prepare bancha tea and serve the tea with apple juice in proportions that may vary from 3 parts juice and 7 parts tea to equal parts juice and tea. Add a wedge of lemon if desired. Serve warm or cool for a special treat or cooling summer drink.

Roasted Barley Tea with Apple Juice

Follow package directions for making roasted barley tea or try these proportions.

2 Tbsp. roasted ground barley
6 cups water

Simmer water and barley 5 minutes, let it steep 3 to 5 minutes, then strain. Serve with apple juice and/or lemon wedges.

Hot Carob Mocha

A caffeine-free hot "cocoa" for a warming winter evening or midday snack.

1 heaping tsp. grain coffee
1 tsp. carob powder
½ tsp. barley malt syrup, or to taste
1 tsp. tahini
1 cup boiling water

Mix grain coffee and carob powder in a coffee mug. Add tahini and malt syrup. Pour boiling water into the mug and whisk with a fork to make a frothy drink. Makes 1 serving.

Grain Coffee Latte

1 heaping tsp. grain coffee
⅓ cup vanilla soy milk
1 tsp. carob powder
1 tsp. barley malt syrup, or to taste
⅔ cup boiling water

Mix grain coffee, soy milk, carob powder, and malt syrup in a coffee mug. Pour boiling water over it, stir, and serve.

Desserts

Cakes

Berry Zucchini Cake

8-oz. jar blackberry or blueberry conserves (fruit only, no
   sugar or honey)
¼ to ⅓ cup maple syrup
⅓ cup corn oil
⅓ cup sultana raisins or other raisins
1 tsp. vanilla extract
4 to 4⅓ cups shredded fresh zucchini
2 to 2½ tsp. brown rice vinegar
3 Tbsp. grated lemon rind
3 cups whole wheat flour or whole wheat pastry flour
¼ tsp. salt
2 to 2½ tsp. baking soda
⅓ cup chopped walnuts
3 Tbsp. poppy seeds

Preheat oven to 350°F. Lightly oil two 8-inch or 9-inch cake
pans or one 9" x 13" x 2" baking dish. Combine conserves,
maple syrup, oil, raisins, vanilla, zucchini, vinegar and lemon rind and mix with a wooden spoon or fork. Mix flour,
salt, baking soda, walnuts and poppy seeds. Combine liquid
and dry ingredients. Batter should be thicker than cake batter but not as stiff as bread dough. If batter is too runny, add
¼ cup more flour.

Spoon batter into lightly oiled cake pans and bake at
350°F for 1 to 1½ hours. Cake should be lightly browned on
top and cooked through. Test with a toothpick. Cool before
serving. Extra cake may be wrapped and refrigerated.

Carob Beany Cake
Thick, chocolatey-looking cake.

1 to 1¼ cups cooked lentils
⅓ to ½ cup unrefined corn or safflower oil
¾ cup sorghum or barley malt syrup
1 to 1½ tsp. pure vanilla extract
½ cup carob powder
4 Tbsp. flaxseed
¾ cup boiling water
½ cup warm water
1¾ to 2 cups whole wheat pastry flour
½ cup unbleached wheat flour or rice flour
¼ tsp. salt
1½ tsp. baking soda
1 tsp. cinnamon
½ cup raisins or sultanas
½ cup walnuts, chopped (optional)

Press cooked lentils through a sieve or strainer with a wooden spoon. Add oil, sorghum or malt syrup, vanilla, and carob.

Grind flaxseed in a coffee mill or blender. Pour boiling water over flaxseed meal and let it sit 15 minutes. Whisk with a fork, wire whisk, or blender.

Preheat oven to 375°F. Lightly oil an 8-inch square baking pan. Add flaxseed binder and warm water to the lentil and carob mixture. Combine flours, salt, and baking soda; add to other mixture. Stir in raisins and walnuts. Mixture should resemble fudge brownie batter. Pour into pan and bake at 375°F for approximately 1 hour.

Variation:

– Carob Brownies: Substitute 2 cups Chestnut Raisin
Mousse (page 252) or 2 cups Azuki Raisin Puree (page
261) for lentil-sorghum mixture. Reduce or omit sorghum
or barley malt syrup, and adjust quantities of flour and liquids for desired fudgy or cakey consistency.

Azuki Bean Chestnut Cake

3 Tbsp. ground flaxseed
9 Tbsp. boiling water
1 cup Chestnut Puree (page 262)
¼ cup light sesame oil or corn oil
2 cups Azuki Raisin Puree (page 261)
1 tsp. cinnamon
1 cup rice flour or whole wheat flour
½ cup oat flour or barley flour
¼ cup carob powder (optional)
1 tsp. vanilla

Soak flaxseed in boiling water 15 minutes, then whisk well.
Mix chestnut puree, oil, and azuki raisin puree together.
Add flaxseed mixture. Sift dry ingredients together and add
with vanilla to liquid ingredients. Pour batter into two lightly oiled 9-inch cake pans or one oblong pan. Bake at 350°F
for 1 to 1¼ hours.

Wheat-Free Carob Cake

- 1⅔ cups corn flour
- ⅔ cup barley flour
- 2 tsp. baking powder
- ¼ tsp. baking soda
- ½ tsp. or less sea salt
- 1 tsp. cinnamon
- ½ cup carob powder
- 1½ cups vanilla soy milk
- ⅓ cup maple syrup or rice syrup
- ¼ to ½ cup oil
- ¼ cup water or apple juice

Preheat oven to 350°F. Lightly oil one 9-inch round or square cake pan. Sift dry ingredients, then set aside. Mix wet ingredients in a separate bowl.

Mix liquids and dry ingredients together, then whisk with a fork. Pour into pan and bake for 35 to 40 minutes or until toothpick inserted in middle comes out clean. When cool, run knife around edges of pan. It should turn out onto a plate easily.

Frost with Carob Chestnut Cream Frosting, Maple Tofu Cream Frosting, Amasake Frosting, or Mocha Whip Frosting. Or spoon Cranberry Applesauce, Applesauce, or diluted Amasake Rice Pudding over each piece.

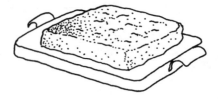

Carob Chip Snackin' Cake

2¼ cup whole wheat pastry flour
¼ cup rice flour
½ cup rolled oats or oat flour
¼ tsp. sea salt
½ tsp. baking soda
2 tsp. baking powder
1½ cups vanilla soy milk
½ cup water
⅔ cup rice syrup
⅓ to ½ cup safflower oil
1 tsp. vanilla extract (optional)
⅓ cup chopped walnuts
1 cup carob chips or raisins

Preheat oven to 350 °F. Lightly oil a 9" x 13" baking pan. Sift dry ingredients and set aside. Mix wet ingredients in a bowl.

Mix wet and dry ingredients together. Add walnuts and carob chips and mix well. Pour into pan and bake 30 minutes or until golden on top and a toothpick inserted in the center comes out clean.

Frost with Maple Tofu Cream Frosting sprinkled with carob chips, Carob Chestnut Cream Frosting, or Carob Frosting. Or pour amasake puree over each piece. Or glaze with Rice Malt Kuzu Glaze or Raisin Sauce.

Coffee Cake

- ¼ cup instant grain coffee
- 3¾ cups whole wheat pastry flour
- 2 tsp. baking powder
- 1 tsp. baking soda
- ½ cup corn oil
- ¾ cup rice syrup
- 1 Tbsp. vanilla extract
- 1¾ cups water
- 2 Tbsp. brown rice vinegar or cider vinegar

Ripple mixture:

- 1 cup rolled oats
- 1 Tbsp. cinnamon
- 3 pinches sea salt
- ½ cup tahini
- ¼ cup chopped raisins or ¼ cup walnuts, cut into pieces
- 1 cup apple juice

Preheat oven to 350°F. Lightly oil a 9-inch square baking pan. Prepare ripple mixture and set aside. Sift dry ingredients together. Combine liquid ingredients and add to dry ingredients. Stir well with a whisk.

Pour half the cake batter into lightly oiled baking pan. Sprinkle half of the ripple mixture on top. Add the rest of the cake batter and top with remaining ripple mixture. Bake at 350°F for 40 to 55 minutes or until golden on top.

Couscous Fruit Cake

6 cups apple cider
6 cups water
2 cups raisins
sea salt
2½ cups couscous
1 Tbsp. vanilla or almond extract
1 to 2 tsp. cinnamon (optional)
¼ cup chopped almonds or walnuts, roasted
2 Tbsp. sesame tahini or sesame butter

Bring cider, water, raisins, and a pinch of salt to a boil. Add couscous, reduce heat, cover, and simmer over low heat for 15 minutes or until most of liquid is absorbed and couscous has expanded.

Turn off heat, mix in vanilla or almond extract, cinnamon if desired, nuts, and tahini. Spoon into two 9-inch square pans.

Let cool until mixture sets, then cut into squares.

Tips:

– Serve as a snack or breakfast dish.

– This will keep at room temperature for 2 to 3 days. Refrigerate after that time; it will keep 6 to 8 days.

Couscous Layer Cake
Needs no baking.

6 cups apple juice
2 to 3 cups water
1 cup raisins
2 to 3 pinches sea salt
3 cups couscous
1 tsp. vanilla or almond extract

Boil apple juice with 2 cups water, raisins, and salt. Add couscous, stir, reduce heat, cover pot, and stir occasionally. Cook about 15 minutes or until mixture is very thick. Add up to 1 more cup water during cooking if necessary.

Turn off heat, add vanilla or almond extract, and let mixture sit in pot with lid on about 10 minutes. Pour into two 9-inch round cake pans, and spread evenly. Let set several hours or until firm.

Variations:
- This cake can be served without filling, topped with stewed fruit or chopped roasted nuts.

- Add grated lemon peel and a spoonful of sesame butter.

- Frost with Amasake Frosting.

- Glaze with Pecan Malt Glaze.

Date Muffins

2 cups vanilla soy milk
1¼ cups cooked rice
¼ cup safflower oil
⅔ to 1 cup chopped dates
1 tsp. vinegar
½ cup water
1 cup brown rice flour
⅓ cup oat flour
⅔ cup buckwheat flour
1 tsp. cinnamon
1¼ tsp. baking soda
¼ tsp. sea salt

Preheat oven to 325°F. Prepare muffin pans with paper liners. Blend soy milk, rice, oil, dates, vinegar, and water in blender. Combine dry ingredients in a bowl. Add the liquid mixture to the dry ingredients and mix well.

Pour into paper muffin cup liners in muffin pans. Bake at 325° to 350°F for 18 to 25 minutes or until golden on top.

Tips:

– Use 1 cup raisins in place of dates.

– Make your own oat and buckwheat flour in a coffee mill. Rice flour should be purchased or milled more finely.

– Flash freeze muffins in ziplock bags while hot out of the oven to retain moisture. They will taste fresh when defrosted.

Gingerbread Cake

¼ to ½ cup oil
1½ cups water or soy milk
⅔ cup barley malt syrup or blackstrap molasses
2 to 2¼ cups whole wheat pastry flour
½ tsp. sea salt
1 tsp. soda
½ tsp. cinnamon
¼ tsp. nutmeg
2 tsp. dry ginger powder

Preheat oven to 350°F. Lightly oil a 9-inch square baking pan. Whip oil, water, and barley malt syrup or molasses with a whisk. Sift flour, salt, baking soda, and spices. Combine liquid and dry ingredients, continuing to whisk.

Pour or spoon mixture into lightly oiled baking pan. Bake at 350°F for 35 to 40 minutes.

Frost with Tofu Cream Frosting, or top with amasake or applesauce.

Gingerbread Coffee Cake

3¾ cups whole wheat pastry flour
2 tsp. baking powder
¾ tsp. sea salt
1½ tsp. ginger powder
3 Tbsp. grain coffee powder
⅔ cup or less oil
½ cup water
1½ cups or less barley malt or molasses
2 Tbsp. cider vinegar
1 cup soy milk

Preheat oven to 350°F. Lightly oil two 9-inch cake pans. Mix dry ingredients and wet ingredients separately, then mix all together. Pour or spoon into lightly oiled baking pans. Bake at 350°F for 30 to 45 minutes or until toothpick inserted in the middle comes out clean.

Ginger Cake

A delightful, light, dairy-free, egg-free, and sugar-free cake.

- 2½ cups whole wheat pastry flour
- ½ tsp. sea salt
- 2 tsp. baking powder
- 1 cup barley malt or maple syrup
- ½ cup corn oil
- 1 tsp. vanilla extract
- 1 tsp. fresh ginger juice (grate ginger root and squeeze it in your fist into a spoon)
- 1 cup grain coffee (1 to 2 tsp. powder to 1 cup water)
- ½ tsp. cinnamon
- ½ tsp. allspice

Preheat oven to 375°F. Lightly oil a 9-inch cake pan or prepare muffin pans with paper liners for 12 to 16 muffins. Sift flour, salt, and baking powder together. In a separate bowl, mix remaining ingredients together.

Gradually add dry ingredients to liquid ingredients, mixing well after each addition. Pour into muffin pans or cake pan. Bake at 375°F for 30 minutes or until a toothpick inserted in the center of cake comes out clean. Muffins may cook more quickly.

Cool before cutting or frosting with Mocha Whip Frosting.

Lemon Cake

- ½ cup lemon juice (juice of 2 lemons)
- ⅓ to ½ cup light corn, safflower, or sesame oil
- ⅔ cup plus 2 Tbsp. rice syrup
- 2½ tsp. fresh ginger juice
- 1½ tsp. cider vinegar or rice vinegar
- ⅔ cup vanilla soy milk
- ¼ tsp. sea salt
- 2 tsp. vanilla
- 2 cups sifted whole wheat pastry flour
- 2 tsp. baking soda
- 3 Tbsp. poppy seeds

Preheat oven to 350°F. Lightly oil a 9-inch square baking pan. Whisk lemon juice, oil, syrup, ginger juice, vinegar, and soy milk with a wire whisk or fork. Slowly add salt, vanilla, flour, and baking soda, whisking continuously. Add poppy seeds. Pour mixture into baking pan. Bake for 35 to 40 minutes or until it tests done with a toothpick. Frost with Tofu Cream Frosting.

Miso Fruit Cake

2⅔ to 3¼ cups raisins
3 to 3⅓ cups apple juice or apple cider
3½ cups whole wheat flour or pastry flour
½ cup corn oil
2 tsp. vanilla
2 Tbsp. white, mellow, yellow, or sweet rice miso
3 cups grated apple
2 Tbsp. fresh lemon juice
2 to 3 tsp. grated lemon rind
1 cup sunflower seeds, roasted or chopped roasted walnuts

Bring raisins and apple juice or cider to a boil. Simmer, covered, for 45 minutes.

Dry roast flour, stirring constantly, until golden or lightly browned. Set aside.

Mix oil, vanilla, miso dissolved in a bit of apple juice, grated apple, lemon juice and rind, and sunflower seeds. Add raisin and juice mixture, then add flour. Pour or spoon into two lightly oiled 8-inch cake pans or one 9" x 13" pan. Bake at 350°F for 1 hour. Place a pan of water on the bottom shelf of the oven to steam cakes and keep them from drying out while baking.

Allow cakes to cool before cutting. Wrap in plastic or place in a cake tin to retain moistness.

Parsnip Cake

2 tsp. oil
3 pounds parsnips, cut finely
1 pinch sea salt
4 cups apple juice
vanilla extract, to taste
1 large lemon, halved and squeezed for juice
1 Tbsp. sesame butter or tahini
1 Tbsp. barley malt or rice syrup (optional)
1½ cups couscous

Saute parsnips in oil with salt over medium heat for 10 minutes.

Pour 2 cups of the apple juice into pressure cooker. Add parsnips and pressure cook 40 minutes or until soft. Put mixture through food mill or blender.

While parsnips are cooking, mix vanilla with remaining apple juice in a bowl. Add lemon juice, sesame butter, and a little salt, if desired. Stir in barley malt or rice syrup and couscous.

Mix parsnips with other ingredients. Bake in oiled 9" x 13" x 2" cake pan at 350°F for 1 hour.

Poppyseed Cake

3 cups whole wheat pastry flour
2 tsp. baking soda
½ tsp. sea salt
⅓ to ½ cup corn oil
1 cup rice syrup
1 Tbsp. vanilla essence
1 lemon, juiced
8.5 oz. vanilla soy milk
1 tsp. cinnamon
3 Tbsp. poppy seeds
1 tsp. brown rice vinegar

Preheat oven to 375°F. Lightly oil two 9-inch cake pans or prepare muffin pans with liners for 24 muffins. Sift flour, soda, and salt or mix together. In a separate bowl, mix remaining ingredients.

Mix wet ingredients with dry ingredients and stir with a whisk to mix well. Spoon into muffin pans or pour into cake pans. Bake at 375°F for 35 to 55 minutes or until golden. Muffins cook more quickly than cakes. Store muffins in airtight containers to retain freshness.

Tofu Cheesecake

Granola Crust:

- ¾ cup whole wheat pastry flour
- ¾ cup rolled oats
- ¼ tsp. sea salt
- 1 Tbsp. maple syrup or rice syrup (optional)
- ¼ cup corn oil
- 2 Tbsp. apple juice or water
- ¼ cup roasted sesame seeds

Mix dry ingredients. Add oil and liquids. Oil pie pan, and pat dough on bottom and sides of pan. Bake at 350°F for 10 minutes.

Filling:

- 1 lb. firm or silken tofu
- ½ cup maple syrup or ¾ to 1 cup rice syrup
- ½ cup tahini
- 1 tsp. vanilla
- juice of ½ lemon

Blend ingredients in a blender. Pour mixture into pie crust and bake at 350°F for 30 minutes.

Topping:

- 1 cup apple juice
- 2 Tbsp. maple syrup or rice syrup (optional)
- ½ Tbsp. arrowroot diluted in ½ Tbsp. apple juice
- 2 cups fruit (dark cherries work well)

Heat juice. Add sweetener and diluted arrowroot; cook until thick. Add fruit at the end. Spread over baked cheesecake.

Mim Collins-Drewry

Light Lemony Tofu Cheesecake

1½ lbs. soft or firm tofu (not vacuum-packed)
1 cup rice syrup
1 pinch sea salt
¼ cup corn oil, light sesame oil, or tahini
1½ to 2 tsp. vanilla
2 to 3 Tbsp. lemon juice
⅔ to 1 cups water
2 Tbsp. kuzu or arrowroot dissolved in cold water
2 to 3 cups crumbled lemon snaps or other cookies.
Very Berry Topping (page 261, optional)

Puree all ingredients except the cookie crumbs and topping in a blender until smooth. Press cookie crumbs on bottom and sides of a 9-inch pie pan. Pour tofu filling into crumb crust. Bake at 350°F for 30 to 40 minutes. Let cool and spread with topping if desired.

Cookies

Buckwheat Apple Brownies
A wheat-free, dairy-free delight sweetened with fruit.

1 to 1¼ cups buckwheat flour
1 tsp. baking soda
½ tsp. cinnamon
¼ cup light oil (sesame, corn, or safflower)
½ to ¾ cup apple juice
1 cup cooked applesauce
½ cup liquid left over from cooking potatoes or 2 Tbsp.
   kuzu dissolved in ½ cup cold water
2 tsp. brown rice vinegar or cider vinegar

Preheat oven to 350°F. Lightly oil a 9-inch square pan. Mix flour, baking soda, and cinnamon; set aside. Mix oil, apple juice, and applesauce. Add potato starch liquid or kuzu diluted in water. Add to flour mixture, stir, then add vinegar. Bake in lightly oiled 9-inch square pan at 350°F for 35 minutes or until done.

Variation:
– In place of applesauce use cooked pears and raisins, or stewed dried apples.

Amasake Oatmeal Cookies

1¼ cups whole wheat flour
3 to 4 pinches sea salt
2¼ cups rolled oats
1 tsp. baking soda
2 tsp. rice vinegar or cider vinegar
2 cups amasake
1 tsp. cinnamon
¼ cup barley malt syrup
¼ cup rice syrup
½ to ¾ cup raisins or sultanas
¼ to ½ cup chopped almonds or walnuts

Preheat oven to 350°-375°F. Lightly oil a cookie sheet. Mix flour, salt, oats, and soda. Add vinegar, amasake, cinnamon, syrups, raisins, and chopped nuts; mix well. Mixture should be of cookie-dough consistency. Adjust liquid if necessary.

Drop 1 to 2 tablespoons of batter on sheet to make each cookie. Bake 12 to 15 minutes or until lightly golden on the underside and on top.

Suggestions:

– Cookies can be frozen immediately in ziplock bags and then thawed for a just-baked taste. This "flash-freezing" technique requires that you freeze them before they cool, so they retain all their moisture.

– You can use sweet rice amasake, barley and rice amasake, or just rice amasake. I do not recommend using millet and sweet rice amasake, buckwheat amasake, or roasted barley amasake, as their tastes would be too overpowering.

Butter Pecan Cookies

1 Tbsp. flaxseed meal (optional)
6 Tbsp. boiling water (optional)
⅓ cup sesame butter or tahini
⅓ cup corn oil or light sesame oil
½ to ¾ cup maple syrup; or a combination of rice syrup and
    barley malt
¼ tsp. sea salt
1 tsp. baking soda
2 cups flour: 1 cup whole wheat flour or whole wheat pastry
    flour and 1 cup unbleached flour; or 1½ cups whole
    wheat flour and ½ cup unbleached flour
½ tsp. vanilla
½ to ⅔ cup unsweetened flaked coconut
½ cup chopped roasted pecans

Preheat oven to 350°F. Prepare flaxseed binder, if desired, by soaking flaxseed meal in boiling water for 15 minutes. Combine remaining ingredients. Whisk flaxseed binder well and add to mixture.

Form into tablespoon-sized balls and place on a lightly-oiled baking sheet. Press with tines of a fork to make a cross-hatching design on top of cookies. Bake at 350°F for 12 to 15 minutes, or until underside is lightly browned but not burned.

Variation:

– For a less-rich cookie, omit the oil and use ⅓ cup or less sweetener. Increase liquid as needed for cookie-dough consistency.

Ginger Snaps or Gingerbread People

- 1¾ cup barley flour or whole wheat pastry flour
- ½ tsp. baking soda
- ½ tsp. cinnamon
- ½ cup apple juice concentrate, thawed
- 3-6 Tbsp. blackstrap molasses
- 2 Tbsp. safflower oil
- 1½ to 2 tsp. grated fresh ginger root

Preheat oven to 350°F. Sift together flour, baking soda, and cinnamon. Cream together juice, molasses, and oil. Stir in ginger. Add wet to dry ingredients and mix well.

Roll out dough on a lightly floured wooden board. Cut with cookie cutters and transfer to oiled cookie sheet. Bake 8 to 10 minutes, watching carefully. Remove from oven while still soft, as ginger snaps will harden as they cool.

Emily Bader

Linzer Torte Cookies

1 cup almonds, ground very fine
1 cup oat flour
2 tsp. baking powder
½ tsp. cinnamon
pinch salt (optional)
⅓ cup rice syrup
2 Tbsp. barley malt
⅓ cup safflower oil
½ cup unsweetened raspberry jam

Preheat oven to 350°F. Combine dry ingredients in a large mixing bowl. Cream together sweeteners and oil. Add wet to dry ingredients.

Form walnut-sized balls. Placed on oiled baking sheets. Press down in center using thumb to form an indentation. Place ½ teaspoon jam in each center. Bake 10 to 15 minutes or until golden.

Emily Bader

Oatmeal Cookies

⅔ cup raisins
⅔ cup water
1 cup whole wheat pastry flour
2⅔ cups rolled oats
⅛ tsp. sea salt
1 tsp. baking soda
¼ tsp. cinnamon
⅓ cup oil
2 tsp. rice vinegar
⅔ cup rice syrup

Bring raisins and water to a boil; reduce heat and simmer 15 minutes. Set aside.

Preheat oven to 375°F. Lightly oil a cookie sheet. Mix flour, oats, sea salt, baking soda, and cinnamon. Combine raisins, water, oil, vinegar and rice syrup. Mix liquid and dry ingredients together.

Place large tablespoon-sized balls of dough on sheet and flatten. Bake 10 to 15 minutes or until golden. Remove from cookie sheet and cool on a wire rack. They will become more crisp as they cool. Store in a cookie jar or tin, or wrap in plastic for a portable snack. Makes 15 large or 24 small cookies.

Sweet Rice Cookies

- ⅔ to 1 cup rolled oats
- 1 cup brown rice flour
- 3 pinches sea salt
- ½ tsp. baking soda
- ⅓ cup raisins
- ⅛ to ¼ cup oil
- 1¼ cups amasake concentrate (homemade or store-bought)
- ½ tsp. cider vinegar or rice vinegar

Preheat oven to 325°F. Lightly oil a baking sheet. Mix oats, flour, salt, and soda. Add raisins, oil, amasake, and vinegar. Stir. Drop onto lightly oiled baking sheet and bake at 325°F for 10 to 15 minutes, or until golden. Makes 8 to 10 medium-sized cookies.

Raisin Rye Cookies

½ cup water
½ cup raisins
1⅔ cup rye flour
1 cup rolled oats
¼ tsp. ginger powder
⅛ tsp. cinnamon
dash allspice
2 to 3 pinches salt
⅓ cup corn oil or safflower oil
½ to ⅔ cup barley malt syrup

Boil water and raisins 5 to 10 minutes or until almost all the liquid is absorbed. Preheat oven to 375°F. Oil a cookie sheet. Blend dry ingredients and add raisins and water with oil and syrup. Mix well. It should form a big ball of dough.

Pinch off large teaspoon-sized pieces of dough and roll between your hands to form balls. Place on cookie sheet and press with your thumb or bottom of a glass to flatten cookies. Bake 12 to 15 minutes. Remove from cookie sheet and let cool. Makes 20 to 24 small cookies.

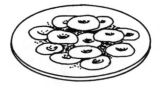

Rice Crispy Treats

- 1 Tbsp. light corn, sesame, or safflower oil
- 2 Tbsp. tahini or almond butter
- ¾ cup barley malt syrup
- ¾ cup rice syrup (or use 1½ cup rice syrup and omit barley malt)
- 2 tsp. vanilla or almond extract
- 1 box (10 oz.) brown rice crispy cereal
- 8 rice cakes, crumbled
- 1 cup raisins

In heavy skillet mix oil, tahini or almond butter, and syrup and heat until it bubbles. Remove from heat and add vanilla or almond extract and stir. Add cereal, rice cakes, and raisins; mix well to coat. Spread and press onto cookie sheet or cake pans. Let cool. Slice.

Rice Malt Crunch Balls

- a few drops vegetable oil
- ¾ to 1 cup rice syrup or mixture of equal parts barley malt and rice syrup or rice malt
- ¼ cup sesame butter, tahini, or nut butter
- 2 tsp. almond extract
- 8-oz. package rice cakes, crumbled
- ½ cup raisins

Brush saucepan with just enough oil to make it shiny. Add rice syrup and nut butter, and cook over medium heat 3 to 5 minutes or until mixture bubbles. Turn off burner to avoid scorching.

Add almond extract and immediately add crumbled rice

cakes and raisins. Mix well to coat the rice cake pieces. Add more rice cakes if you have extra syrup. Rice cake pieces should be well-coated but not overly syrupy or gooey.

Place mixture in a baking dish and bake at 350°F for 5 to 7 minutes. Watch so mixture doesn't get too browned and crisp, as it will harden some after it cools. Remove from oven and as soon as mixture becomes cool enough to handle, oil hands and form mixture into balls. Allow balls to cool and harden, then wrap each in a plastic bag or wax paper.

Variations:

– Use puffed millet, puffed barley, puffed corn, or other puffed cereal.

– Use round oat cereal or crisp rice cereal.

– Use less nut butter and mix in chopped roasted peanuts, almonds, or sunflower seeds with the raisins and cereal.

– Press cereal mixture onto a cookie sheet or into an oblong pan, bake 5 to 7 minutes, then let cool and cut into squares. Leftover squares may be stored in an airtight jar.

Pies and Puddings

Fruit Pie

1¼ cups raisins
2¼ cups dried nectarines, cut up
3 cups water
pinch sea salt
7 cups organic red apples (with or without peels) cut in ¼-inch wedges
2 cups water
1 tsp. cinnamon (optional)
3 Tbsp. kuzu or arrowroot powder
¼ cup cold water
2 unbaked pie shells

Soak raisins and nectarines in 3 cups water with salt for 30 minutes. Add to a pot with apples, 2 cups water, and cinnamon, if desired. Boil 30 to 40 minutes until tender.

Dissolve kuzu or arrowroot powder in ¼ cup cold water and add to boiling fruit mixture. Stir and cook until thickened 1 to 2 minutes, then turn off heat. Pour into unbaked pie shells and bake at 325°F for 30 minutes.

Serving Suggestion:

– Omit pie shells and serve as fruit compote with or without baking it for ½ hour in a casserole dish.

Couscous Dessert Balls

To make 30 1-inch balls:

2½ cups apple juice
1½ cups water
2 cups couscous
1 to 2 pinches sea salt
1 to 1⅓ cups almonds, walnuts, or pecans
1 tsp. vanilla or almond essence

To make 50 1-inch balls:

3¾ cups apple juice
1¾ cups water
3 cups couscous
2 pinches sea salt
1½ to 2 cups almonds, walnuts, or pecans
1¼ tsp. vanilla or almond essence

Bring juice, water, couscous, and salt to a boil. Cover and cook over low heat 10 to 12 minutes or until liquid is absorbed.

While couscous is cooking, dry-roast almonds, walnuts, or pecans. Rinse them in a strainer, then place on a baking sheet in a 200° to 250°F oven. Stir the nuts occasionally and watch them so they do not burn. Roast 8 to 12 minutes. They will smell very nutty and be lightly golden when done; do not over roast. Remove nuts from pan immediately, and pour nuts into a large bowl. Reserve one nut half to put on top of each ball. Chop the remainder of the nuts.

Remove couscous from heat and stir in chopped nuts and vanilla or almond essence. Let pot sit, covered, for 10 minutes, then spoon into a large glass bowl. Fluff it up a bit so it is not packed.

Wet hands and have a bowl of cold water on the counter to dip your hands in. Make 1-inch couscous balls and place them on a plate or serving platter with 1 toasted nut half on top of each ball. Serve them as desserts, snacks, or breakfast treats glazed with Rice Malt Kuzu Glaze; spoon 1 heaping teaspoonful of glaze over each couscous ball. The balls can be kept for up to a week in the refrigerator or 1 to 2 days at room temperature.

Variation:

– Form couscous mixture into several small cakes using bowls or glass molds and let them set. Then turn out on a plate and glaze them. Top with several roasted nuts.

Arlene's Steamed Apricot Pudding

½ cup sesame seeds
½ cup roasted sunflower seeds
¾ cup flaxseed meal
1 tsp. kelp powder
9-oz. jar natural apricot conserves

Mix ingredients. Spoon into a can or bowl that can be placed in a larger pot for steaming. Tie waxed paper over the top, and steam 3 hours. Serve at room temperature.

Arlene Quamme

Nut or Seed Pancakes

1½ cups nut or seed meal (almond, pecan, or sunflower)
½ cup flaxseed meal
1 tsp. baking powder or soda
¼ tsp. sea salt (optional)
1 cup liquid (soy milk, apple juice, or amasake)
¼ cup or less sunflower, almond, apricot, or other oil
1 egg substitute (mix 1½ Tbsp. flaxseed meal with 3 Tbsp. boiling water; let sit and whisk)

Combine dry ingredients and mix well. Combine wet ingredients and add them to the dry ingredients, mixing gently. If batter thickens, add a small amount of liquid, as needed, to make a pourable liquid. Make small pancakes and cook on a lightly-oiled cast iron or stainless griddle or skillet.

Banana Cream Pie

Bananas are generally not eaten on a macrobiotic diet in a temperate climate because they are tropical. This is a special occasion dish.

4 medium bananas, sliced
1⅔ cup soy milk, plain or vanilla-flavored
2 pinches sea salt
1 cup clear seitan starch water and
1½ cups thick seitan starch (left over from making Seitan, page 148)
3 Tbsp. almond butter
2 Tbsp. rice syrup
1½ tsp. vanilla
14 to 16 rice malt-sweetened cookies

Place bananas, soy milk, salt, seitan starch and water, almond butter, and rice syrup in a pot. Bring to a boil, then simmer over medium heat 15 minutes, stirring well. Add vanilla and stir.

Break several whole cookies in half to line the side of a 9-inch pie pan. Crush the remaining cookies and line the bottom of the pan with the crumbs. Pour in banana filling, cover, and chill.

Notes and Variations:

– Seitan starch water is the water saved from the first rinsing when making seitan. Once the starch water settles, you can pour off some of the clear liquid and use the milky thick starch.

– Use sugar-free granola for the crust, in place of cookies.

Candied Yam Pie

4 cups apple juice
2 cups water
7 yams, medium size, scrubbed well
2 cups cut carrots
2 Tbsp. corn, safflower, or light sesame oil
½ tsp. sea salt
1 tsp. cinnamon
½ tsp. ginger powder
⅓ cup rice syrup (optional)
1½ to 2 Tbsp. kuzu or arrowroot powder
¼ to ⅓ cup apple juice or cold water
1 tsp. vanilla extract (optional)
pie crust for 2 pie shells

Bring juice and water to a boil; add yams. Cover and simmer over medium heat 10 minutes. Turn off heat, remove yams, and run cold water over them to remove peel. Cut yams into pieces and set aside. Save the cooking liquid to add back later.

Saute carrots in oil. Add yam pieces, stir, add liquid back to pot and bring mixture to a boil. Simmer over medium to low heat until soft. Add salt, cinnamon, and ginger as soon as carrots and yams are simmering. They should be soft within 20 to 30 minutes.

Blenderize the vegetable mixture, or puree in a food mill, to make a creamy, custard-like consistency, adding rice syrup, if desired. Dissolve kuzu in apple juice or cold water, and mix into yam and carrot puree while it is still warm. Add vanilla, if desired.

Prepare pie crust and pre-bake it for 10 minutes at 350° to 375°F. Add yam/carrot puree and bake 15 to 20 minutes or until set. Let cool and serve or chill.

Variations:

– Serve as a pudding or a side dish with hot cereal for breakfast.

– Make a Granola Crust (page 214).

Pie Crust for Fruit Tarts or Custards

½ cup whole wheat pastry flour
1 cup graham flour
½ to ⅔ cup rice syrup
½ cup wheat germ
1 cup cold water
½ cup tahini

Mix all ingredients with a fork, then blend with your hands
to form a smooth dough.

Oil two 9-inch pie plates and separate dough into two
balls. Press and spread dough into pie plates to thinly cover
the bottom and sides. Poke bottom of crust with a fork to
make tiny holes.

Fill with fruit pie filling and bake at 325°F for 30 minutes
or until lightly golden. Let cool, or chill pies in refrigerator,
then slice and serve.

Steamed Pudding
This pudding has a rich chocolatey taste.

- 3 to 3½ cups leftover azuki bean rice or chestnut rice combination
- 1½ to 2 Tbsp. tahini or almond butter
- 2 large handfuls raisins
- 1 tsp. vanilla or almond extract
- 1 cup cooked whole oat porridge
- ½ cup rice syrup
- 1½ tsp. cinnamon
- ½ cup flaxseed meal (flaxseed ground in a coffee or spice mill)
- ¼ tsp. sea salt
- ½ cup carob powder

Mix all ingredients. Place in a 16-ounce can or metal pudding bowl, and cover with four layers of wax paper, oiling the first layer which will come in contact with the pudding as it expands. Leave a little room between the top of the bowl and the wax paper. Place several rubber bands around wax paper, or tie it with a string to secure it.

Place can or bowl in a pot with water three-fourths of the way up the side of the can or bowl. Cover the pot, bring to a boil, then reduce heat to medium setting. Cook 5 to 6 hours. Periodically check the pot and add water as needed to keep the pot from drying out and burning.

When pudding is done, cool, remove from can and slice.

Amasake

Amasake is a sweet pudding or drink made from fermented grain and koji. Koji is used to innoculate the grain and to create amasake pudding. Amasake already prepared can be purchased in many natural food stores and macrobiotic specialty shops. It looks like a milkshake and comes in many flavors, in pint containers.

Amasake is a wonderful milk or cream substitute on hot or cold cereal. Use it in cookie or cake recipes, with pancake mixes, or thickened with arrowroot powder, agar agar flakes, or kuzu to make frostings or puddings.

Amasake is sugar-free, honey-free, cholesterol-free and made from whole grain. It is a healthful treat for kids and health enthusiasts.

You can make amasake at home using rice koji, a product available in Japanese grocery stores, some health food stores and co-ops, and macrobiotic stores.

Grain is cooked with more water than usual and removed to glass or ceramic bowls. When the grain has cooled to 130°F or when you can handle it without scalding your hands, purchased koji is added and mixed well. The bowls are covered with warm damp towels and kept in a warm place 6 to 8 hours or overnight. The grain and koji mixture should be kept between 135°F and 140°F but no hotter or the enzymes which break down the starch into sugar will be destroyed. You may want to use a thermometer the first few times you make amasake.

If your oven has a pilot light, you can keep the covered bowls in the oven. If not, you can heat the oven, turn it off, and put the covered bowls in the oven. Then every 2 hours or so, turn the oven on low heat for 10 to 15 minutes; then turn it off.

After the mixture has been kept warm 6 to 8 hours it will be sweet. It is then put in a pot on the stove and a few pinches of salt are added to bring out the sweetness. The amasake is brought to a boil and cooked 8 to 10 minutes over low heat with a heat diffuser under the pot. Stir to prevent burning. The amasake may be cooked for 20 to 25 minutes if you want it to keep longer and be sweeter. The amasake may be pureed in a blender or food mill until smooth. Amasake keeps for up to a week refrigerated in glass jars.

Amasake Pudding

3 cups short-grain brown rice
3 cups pearled or pot barley
8 cups water
7 cups cold water
2 cups organic brown rice koji or white rice koji
4 Tbsp. kuzu
6 Tbsp. water
scant tsp. sea salt

Rinse grains and drain. Pressure cook with 8 cups water for 45 minutes. Remove from pressure cooker and place in two large glass or ceramic bowls. Add 7 cups cold water divided between the two bowls. This will make the grain cool enough so you can add the koji right away and provide enough liquid to keep the koji moist.

Add 1 cup of koji to each bowl and stir well. Cover with a warm, damp kitchen towel and put bowls in a warm place for 8 hours or overnight. Keep the mixture between 135° and 140°F.

After mixture has fermented and become sweet, blend it in a blender. Dissolve kuzu in 6 tablespoons water and add to puree. Put mixture in a pot. Add salt and bring to a low boil, then put a heat diffuser under pot and cook over low heat for 20 minutes. When cool, place in jars and refrigerate.

Suggestions:

– This recipe makes about 30 servings. Cut it in half or in thirds, but do remember that the dessert lasts for up to a week and kids love it, too. It packs well in lunches or for trips in small glass jars.

– Make sundaes by layering amasake pudding in parfait glasses with fruit spreads and chopped roasted nuts on top.

– Serve over apple pie.

– Serve with hot cereal.

– Use it to sweeten cookies.

Barley Mocha Pudding

Has a very rich, chocolatey-coffee taste.

4 cups barley
8 cups water
½ cup rice koji
kuzu or arrowroot powder (optional)

Roast barley in a dry skillet over low heat 25 to 30 minutes. You may need to do it in two batches in order to toast the barley evenly and not burn it.

Soak barley overnight in water. In the morning, boil it for 1¼ hours. Put a flame deflector under pan after it comes to a boil. Turn off heat and allow it to sit, covered, for 1½ to 2 hours. When barley has cooled to 130°F, add koji. Pour into large glass or ceramic bowls and cover with damp towels.

Keep at 135° to 140°F in warm oven for 8 hours. Puree in blender and cook over low heat for 10 to 15 minutes to stop the fermentation. Thicken if necessary with kuzu.

Serving Suggestions:

– Serve as a dessert with roasted walnuts or almonds.

Barley and Rice Amasake Pudding
A creamy sweet pudding dessert.

2 to 3 cups water
12 cups leftover cooked rice and barley mixture (best if 1 to
    2 days old)
1 heaping cup koji
2 to 4 cups water
few pinches sea salt
kuzu (optional)
ginger juice or vanilla extract (optional)

Heat 2 to 3 cups water and leftover grain in a pot on the stove until it almost boils. Reduce heat to cook at approximately 140° to 150°F. Pour into a large glass bowl and let cool until you can handle it with your hands without getting burned (130°F). Then add koji, stir, cover with a warm, damp kitchen towel, and place in a warm area for 6 to 8 hours or overnight. Keep the rice and koji mixture between 135° and 140°F.

After the amasake has fermented 6 to 8 hours or overnight, place it in a pot on the stove and add 2 to 4 cups water. Bring it to a low boil, then cook it over low heat for 8 to 10 minutes, stirring to prevent burning. Add a few pinches of salt while it is cooking to help bring out the sweetness. Add ginger juice or vanilla if desired. Let cool, then puree in a blender or hand food mill until smooth. Dilute with water or thicken with kuzu if desired. Refrigerate in jars and serve as a dessert, or use in cookies, breads, muffins, or cupcakes as a sweetener.

Millet and Sweet Rice Amasake
Has a very rich, sweet, marshmallow-like taste.

2 cups sweet brown rice
1 cup millet
4 cups water
3 cups cold water
¾ cup koji
¼ tsp. sea salt

Put rice, millet and 4 cups water in a pressure cooker and cook 50 minutes. Remove from heat and pour mixture into a large glass or ceramic bowl. Immediately add 3 cups cold water and stir well. Add koji and stir well. Place in a warm oven or near a radiator for 8 hours or overnight to allow it to ferment and get sweet. Then puree in a blender until smooth. Add ¼ teaspoon salt and cook over low heat 8 to 10 minutes, stirring well to prevent burning. Cook longer, 20 to 25 minutes, if you want the amasake to keep longer and be sweeter. Refrigerate and serve for dessert as a pudding, or use in baking if desired.

Serving Suggestions:
– Stir amasake into morning oatmeal for a nice sweet taste, and add a few raisins if desired.

Wheat Berry Rice Amasake Pudding

4 cups water
8 cups cooked rice and wheat berry mixture
1 cup koji
1 cup water
2 Tbsp. kuzu dissolved in 1 cup cold water (optional)
⅛ to ¼ tsp. sea salt

Add water to cooked grain and heat on top of stove. Turn off and pour into glass or ceramic bowls. Let cool to 130°F or until you can touch it and not be scalded. Add koji, stir, then allow mixture to sit in warm place 6 to 8 hours or overnight.

Puree mixture in a blender with 1 cup water. Place in a pot on the stove. If the pudding needs to be thickened, add kuzu and water mixture. Add salt to mixture and cook over low heat 20 minutes, stirring to avoid burning. Refrigerate and serve as a pudding, or use in baking as a sweetener.

Fruit and Vegetable Desserts

Dried Apple Compote

Great when fresh apples are not readily available.

> 6 cups dried apples
> 8 cups water
> ⅛ tsp. sea salt
> ½ to 1½ tsp. cinnamon
> 2 Tbsp. kuzu or arrowroot powder
> ½ cup cold water

Soak dried apples in 8 cups water for 3 hours. Cover and boil with salt and cinnamon for 1 hour. Turn off heat and let mixture sit, covered, 30 minutes.

Dilute kuzu in ½ cup cold water, and add to cooked apple mixture. Bring to a boil and stir well to thicken. Simmer 5 to 6 minutes. Turn off heat and let mixture cool. Serve as is or puree for a smooth applesauce.

Granola Apple Crisp

> 3 cups natural granola
> 8 apples, cored and sliced or chopped
> 1 cup grated mochi
> 1 cup apple juice
> 1 cup water
> ½ tsp. cinnamon (optional)

Spread granola in the bottom of a 9" x 14" x 2" pan. Layer apples on top, followed by mochi. Pour apple juice and water over mochi. Sprinkle top with cinnamon, if desired. Cover and bake 20 minutes at 350°F, or bake uncovered for 15 minutes. Makes 10 servings.

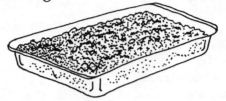

Tips:

– Make your own Granola or use a sugar- and honey-free granola. Most granola is very high in fats (especially saturated fats like palm kernel oil or coconut oil), and sometimes hydrogenated oils. Try finding a natural granola made from rolled oats, dates, sesame seeds, and sunflower seeds only.

Quick Apple Crisp

      several drops vegetable oil
      4 to 5 apples cored, cut in quarters, then in thinner slices
      1 cup oat flakes
      2 to 3 tsp. oil
      2 to 3 handfuls almonds, chopped
      2 to 3 Tbsp. pastry flour
      1 tsp. mirin
      2 to 3 Tbsp. rice syrup
      water

Brush 2 round cake pans with oil. Lay apple pieces in pan in circle arrangements, overlapping pieces slightly.

Mix oat flakes, oil, almonds, flour, mirin, rice syrup and enough water to make a pastelike consistency. Cover apples with mixture. Cover pans and bake at 350°F for 15 to 20 minutes. Uncover and bake another 20 minutes or until golden.

Applesauce

12 apples, peeled, cored, and cut
3 cups water
2 to 3 pinches sea salt
dash cinnamon

Bring ingredients to boil, then simmer, covered, over medium-low heat for 1 to 3 hours. Blenderize or put through a food mill. Serve warm or chilled.

Applesauce in a Flash

5 golden delicious apples, rinsed, cored and cut finely
1½ cups water
½ tsp. cinnamon
⅛ tsp. salt
2 Tbsp. tahini (optional)

Bring apples, water, cinnamon, and salt to a boil. Simmer, covered, over medium heat 15 to 20 minutes, or cook longer for a thicker, sweeter dessert. Stir and mash in the cooking pot, then add tahini if desired and mix again. Serves 6.

Stewed Apricots

- 1¾ cups dried unsulfured Turkish apricots
- 2 cups hot water
- 2 to 3 Tbsp. kuzu or arrowroot
- ½ cup cold water
- ½ tsp. anise or almond extract
- 1 pinch sea salt

Soak apricots in 2 cups water for 1 to 2 hours. Bring to a boil, then simmer, covered, 1 to 2 hours. Dissolve kuzu in cold water. Add to apricot mixture and simmer 5 minutes. Add anise or almond extract and salt. Stir, then chill or cool at room temperature.

Apricot Apple Compote

- 2 cups dried unsulfured Turkish apricots
- 4 cups water
- 6 to 7 medium-sized red apples, peeled, cored, and cut into small pieces
- 1½ cups water
- pinch sea salt
- ¼ tsp. spices, if desired (cinnamon, cloves, nutmeg)
- 1 Tbsp. kuzu or arrowroot powder
- ½ cup cold water

Soak apricots in water 2 hours, or use warm or hot water and soak 30 minutes.

Bring apricots, apple pieces, water, salt, and spices to a boil. Simmer, covered, 1 to 2 hours or until fruits are tender. Dissolve kuzu in cold water and add to fruit mixture. Stir and simmer until thickened.

Cranberry Applesauce

5 large red apples, peeled, cored, and cut
1¼ cups apple juice concentrate
2 pinches sea salt
½ cup agar agar flakes
1¾ cups water
12-oz. package fresh or frozen cranberries

Bring water, apples, apple juice concentrate, and salt to a boil. Cook, covered, over medium heat 15 to 20 minutes. Soften agar agar in water. Add cranberries and agar agar to apples. Return mixture to a boil, then simmer 2 to 3 minutes over medium heat, then over low heat for 5 to 6 minutes. Let cool; blenderize and chill.

Ginger Spiked Pears

6 pears, halved and cored
2 Tbsp. ginger juice, squeezed from grated ginger root
1 Tbsp. barley malt or rice syrup
1 cup water or ½ cup water and ½ cup apple juice

Place pear halves cut side down in a 9" x 13" x 2" baking dish. Squeeze or sprinkle ginger juice over pears. Drizzle barley malt or rice syrup and water over pears.

Cover pan and bake at 350°F for 30 to 35 minutes. Uncover and bake for 5 to 10 minutes.

Tips:
– Prepare this dish ahead by baking 30 minutes. Set aside and reheat 10 to 15 minutes before serving.

Mochi Pear Crisp

3 to 4 pears, cut in quarters, cored, then in thinner slices
2 squares dried mochi, cut finely
1 pinch sea salt
1 handful almonds or walnuts, rinsed and chopped
3 to 4 Tbsp. water

Place pear slices in an overlapping pattern on a 9-inch pie pan. Sprinkle mochi over pears, then salt and water. Top with nuts.

Cover and bake at 300° to 350°F for 20 to 30 minutes. Uncover and bake 10 to 15 minutes until nuts are golden. Slice and serve.

Variations:

– Use apples instead of pears.

– Use pears and apples together.

Squash Pudding

6 cups squash puree
4 cups seitan starch water (left over from making Seitan, page 148)
½ cup roasted ground nuts
2 tsp. cinnamon
½ cup maple syrup or rice syrup (optional)
vanilla to taste

Cook squash puree with starch water, stirring often, until thickened. Add remaining ingredients. Serve as a thick, rich pudding or as a pancake topping.

Pumpkin Pudding

¼ to ½ cup water
5-inch piece kombu
1 kobocha or delicatta squash, cut into chunks
salt or shoyu
soy milk (plain or vanilla), if desired
½ tsp. vanilla or mirin (optional)

Place water and kombu in pot. Layer squash on top and add
a few pinches of salt or season with shoyu near the end of
cooking time. Cook, covered, over low heat for 30 to 45 minutes or until squash is soft. Puree in blender or mash. Add
soy milk or other liquid to make a custard-like pudding.
Add vanilla or mirin if desired, and serve in custard cups.

Tips:
– If the squash is not very sweet, cook with raisins or sultanas, or chop them and add when you puree the squash.

Squash Rings

acorn, butternut or delicatta squash
oil
rice malt
nutmeg
cinnamon

Wash and cut squash into rings. Remove seeds. Place rings on a lightly oiled baking sheet. Lightly brush top sides with rice malt, then sprinkle cinnamon and nutmeg on top. Bake at 375° to 400°F for 45 minutes to 1 hour, or until squash is soft. It helps to place a pan of water on the bottom shelf of oven to prevent squash from drying out.

Gelled Desserts

Apple Apricot Kanten

≡ ½ cup dried apricots
1 cup water
2 cups apple juice
2 Tbsp. agar agar flakes
1 cup cold water
¼ to ½ cup almonds, roasted and chopped (optional)

Soak apricots in water. Combine with apple juice and bring mixture to a boil. Soften agar agar in cold water. Add agar agar to apricots, and simmer about 10 minutes or until agar agar is dissolved. Pour into a rinsed mold and leave at room temperature until cool. Refrigerate until set. Serve garnished with almonds if desired.

Apple Custard

≡ ½ cup agar agar flakes
2 cups apple juice
3 cups water
pinch sea salt
3 Tbsp. tahini
½ tsp. cinnamon (optional)
2 tsp. vanilla or almond extract
chopped roasted almonds (optional)

Place agar agar, juice, water, and salt in pot and let sit 10 minutes. Bring mixture to a boil. Stir in tahini and cinnamon; simmer 6 to 8 minutes or until agar agar flakes are dissolved.

Stir occasionally during cooking. Remove from heat and add vanilla or almond extract.

Let cool. Pour into a bowl and refrigerate several hours or overnight. Puree in blender and serve in individual bowls or goblets. For added texture and richness, garnish each bowl or cup with a teaspoon or two of chopped roasted almonds.

Apple Raisin Walnut Kanten

4 cups apple juice
⅓ cup raisins
1 cup water
4 to 5 apples, cored and cubed
3 to 4 Tbsp. agar agar flakes
1 cup cold water
½ cup walnuts, roasted and chopped

Boil apple juice with raisins and water. Soften agar agar in cold water. Add apples and agar agar to raisins. Simmer 10 to 12 minutes. Pour into serving dishes. Garnish with walnuts. Chill before serving.

Apple Raspberry Parfait

   1 cup dried cherries or raisins
2 cups water

Soak fruit in the water 30 minutes. Set aside.

First layer:

   16-oz. block soft tofu, steamed 10 minutes
2½ cups apple-raspberry juice
⅓ cup agar agar flakes

Blenderize tofu with juice and pour into a pot. Add agar
agar flakes and let sit 10 minutes. Bring to a boil and simmer
over low heat 6 minutes until agar agar flakes are dissolved.
Pour into a glass bowl or mold to half-full. Chill until set.
Then make second layer.

Second layer:

   2 cups apple-raspberry juice or apple-cherry cider
soaked cherries or raisins (from above)
⅓ cup agar agar flakes

Combine juice, soaked fruit and water, and agar agar flakes
in a pot and let sit 10 minutes. Bring mixture to a boil, then
simmer over low heat for 6 to 8 minutes. Allow mixture to
cool slightly and pour over first layer. Chill several hours.
    Turn out onto a plate just before serving. Serves 8 to 10.

Apricot Kanten

- 1 cup dried apricots, cut into pieces
- 3 cups water
- ½ cup apple juice concentrate
- 4 Tbsp. agar agar flakes
- 1 cup cold water

Soak apricots in water until they puff up. Place in saucepan with apple juice concentrate. Bring mixture to a boil. Meanwhile soften agar agar in cold water.

Add agar agar to apricots, and simmer 5 to 8 minutes. Stir to dissolve agar agar. Place mixture in refrigerator to set, or in freezer to set quickly.

Variation:

– Use other dried fruits in place of apricots: peaches, nectarines, pears, apples, or mixed fruits.

Azuki Raisin Pudding

- ¾ cup azuki beans, soaked 6 hours or overnight
- ¾ cup raisins
- 1½ cups water
- 1 cup apple juice
- 2 cups water
- 3 Tbsp. agar agar flakes
- 1 pinch sea salt

Drain azuki beans and discard soaking water. Pressure cook azuki beans, raisins, and 1½ cups fresh water over low heat for 45 to 50 minutes. Add apple juice and 1 cup water; bring mixture to a boil. Soften agar agar in 1 cup water. Add agar agar and salt to azuki bean mixture, and simmer over low heat 8 to 10 minutes until agar agar is dissolved. Pour into dessert mold and let cool. Chill to set.

Cut and serve for dessert, or place in blender and whip or puree. Chill in individual dessert cups.

Chestnut Raisin Mousse

2 cups dried chestnuts
7 cups water
1½ cups apple juice
1 cup raisins
1½ cups cold water
4 to 5 Tbsp. agar agar flakes
1 pinch sea salt
lemon or tangerine slices or grated rind

Soak chestnuts in water overnight. Pour into pressure cooker and pressure cook 45 to 50 minutes. Turn off heat and allow pressure to come down.

Meanwhile, soften agar agar in 1½ cups cold water. Add apple juice, raisins, agar agar, water, and salt to chestnuts. Bring mixture to a boil, then reduce heat and simmer 6 minutes. Remove from heat and let cool 15 minutes.

Pour mixture into a glass dish and chill in the refrigerator to set. To serve, whip in the blender until creamy, then spoon into individual dessert cups and chill.

Serve with a garnish of sliced citrus or grated citrus rind.

Variations:

– After mixture has been simmered, pour into a bundt cake pan or other decorative dish, chill, and turn out onto plate. Slice and serve.

– Experiment with the amount of juice and water to create the desired sweetness and richness. The proportions given are approximations and can easily be changed to suit your taste.

– Use this as a base and sweetener for Carob Brownies.

– Chestnuts can be cooked with azuki beans (1 cup each). Soak each separately overnight, discard bean soak water, then add fresh water and pressure cook 50 minutes.

Blueberry Apple Kanten

1 pint blueberries
3 cups water
3 to 4 Tbsp. agar agar flakes
3 cups apple juice
3 Tbsp. grated lemon rind

Rinse blueberries and spread them in a 9" x 13" x 2" pan. Soften agar agar in 1 cup water. Bring apple juice and 2 cups water to a boil; reduce heat and add agar agar. Simmer 10 to 12 minutes or until agar agar is dissolved. Add lemon rind. Pour mixture over blueberries. Refrigerate 1 hour or more, until mixture is set.

Grain Coffee Aspic Squares

2 cups apple juice
2 Tbsp. instant grain coffee powder
2 cups water
⅓ cup raisins (optional)
¼ cup agar agar flakes
½ tsp. vanilla or almond extract
toasted almonds or peanuts for garnish

In a medium saucepan, combine apple juice and coffee powder with 1 cup water and bring to a boil over moderately high heat. Add raisins if desired. Boil for 10 minutes, stirring occasionally. Soften agar agar in 1 cup water. Add agar agar to apple juice mixture. Simmer for 10 minutes, stirring occasionally, until agar agar is dissolved. Stir in vanilla, remove from heat, and pour into an 8- or 9-inch square pan.

Chill or let set at room temperature. Cut into squares or puree in a blender and top with almonds or peanuts.

Great Grape and Apple Kanten

6 cups apple juice
¾ cup agar agar flakes
3 cups water
rind of 1 lemon, grated
3½ cups fresh grapes

Combine juice, agar agar flakes, and water and let sit for 15 minutes. Bring to a boil and simmer 10 minutes. Add lemon rind and grapes. Pour into large glass bowl and allow it to cool. Place in the refrigerator and let it set for 2 to 3 hours.

Peachy Parfait Pudding

3 cups apple juice
1⅓ cups water
6 Tbsp. agar agar flakes
4 large peaches, peeled and cut finely
1½ to 2 Tbsp. kuzu or arrowroot powder
¼ cup cold water
1 tsp. almond extract
grated rind of ⅓ lemon

Place juice and water in a large pot with agar agar flakes. Let it sit 15 minutes, then bring it to a boil. Reduce heat and simmer 10 minutes or until agar is dissolved. Add peaches.

Dissolve kuzu in cold water, mashing well to dissolve lumps. Add peach mixture, bring to a boil, then reduce heat and cook, stirring, until thickened. Mixture should become translucent within 3 to 4 minutes.

Add almond extract and lemon rind, then remove from heat. Allow mixture to cool at room temperature for 30 to 40 minutes, then refrigerate it to set.

Spoon into individual dessert cups, bowls, or wine glasses for dessert.

Tip:

– This dessert keeps for up to a week in a covered glass dish in your refrigerator.

Dried Pear Aspic

1 cup cold water
½ cup agar agar flakes
1 cup dried pears, finely cut
1 cup hot water
2 cups apple juice
1 pinch sea salt
1 Tbsp. kuzu or arrowroot powder
2 to 3 Tbsp. cold water

Soften agar agar in cold water. Soak pears in hot water 15 to 20 minutes. Add apple juice, agar agar, and salt, then bring mixture to a boil. Reduce heat and simmer 8 to 10 minutes.

Dissolve kuzu in cold water. Add to pear mixture and cook 3 minutes, stirring until thickened. Remove from heat and pour mixture into a mold or glass bowl. Let cool at room temperature, or chill in the refrigerator. It will keep several days, although it is best served fresh.

Variations:
– Dried apricots or raisins can be used in place of pears.

Pear and Pecan Kanten

5 cups boiling water
4 cups dried pears
1 pinch sea salt
6 Tbsp. agar agar flakes
1 cup cold water
1 to 2 cups pecans, chopped

Pour water over pears; let sit for 1 hour. Bring pears and water to a boil. Add salt and simmer 10 minutes. Soften agar agar flakes in cold water and add to pears. Bring to a boil again. Simmer 8 minutes, then turn off heat and let mixture cool.

Roast pecans on a dry baking sheet at 200°F for 15 minutes, stirring well and watching to avoid burning.

Pour pear mixture into glass bowl and chill for 2 to 3 hours. Top with pecans. Serves 12.

Pear and Cinnamon Kanten

6 cups apple juice
4 cups water
1¼ cup agar agar flakes
pinch sea salt
2 pears, cored and cut finely
juice of ½ lemon
¼ tsp. cinnamon
grated rind of ½ lemon

Place apple juice, water, agar agar, and salt in a pot. Let it sit 15 minutes. Meanwhile, cut pears and sprinkle with lemon juice and cinnamon.

Bring apple juice mixture to a boil and simmer 5 minutes. Add pears and lemon rind, and simmer for another 2 to 3 minutes. Pour mixture into a mold or glass bowl. Let cool, then refrigerate until firm. Serves 12 to 15.

Plum Pudding

4 Tbsp. agar agar flakes
4 cups water
3 cups apple juice
pinch sea salt
24 plums, cut finely
2½ to 3 Tbsp. kuzu or arrowroot powder
1 cup cold water
lemon slices

Place agar agar, water, juice, and sea salt in a pot. Let it sit 15 minutes, add plums, and bring mixture to boil. Reduce heat and simmer 10 minutes or until agar agar is dissolved.

Dilute kuzu in cold water and add to pot. Simmer 4 to 5 minutes, stirring, until thickened. Pour into mold or bowl. Let mixture cool for 20 minutes, then refrigerate to set.

Spoon into dessert glasses or bowls and top with a thin slice of lemon.

Raisin Lemon Kanten

1½ cups raisins
5 cups hot water
6 Tbsp. agar agar flakes
1 cup cold water
grated rind from 1 lemon
1 to 1½ Tbsp. rice syrup (optional)

Soak raisins in hot water for 1 hour. Bring to a boil in a covered pot, reduce heat and simmer 8 to 10 minutes. Meanwhile, soften agar agar in cold water. Add agar agar and lemon rind to raisins. Simmer 8 to 10 minutes or until agar

agar is dissolved. Add rice syrup if desired.

Pour into rinsed dish or mold. Chill several hours or overnight. It can also be placed in the freezer for 1 hour for a quick set. Slice and serve.

Marbled Vanilla Raisin Custard

2 cups raisins
4 cups water
1 cup agar agar flakes
1 liter vanilla soy milk

Soak raisins in water 2 to 3 hours. (You can use hot water and soak a shorter period of time, or soak them overnight in refrigerator.) Add agar agar flakes and boil 4 minutes, then reduce heat to medium and slowly add soy milk. Stir well. Simmer 6 minutes, then remove from heat. Separation between water and soy milk may occur.

Let mixture cool 10 minutes, then pour into a glass mold or bowl and chill. Serve in glass bowls or cups. For a creamier consistency, puree in blender after the mixture sets, then transfer to individual serving bowls and chill 1 hour before serving.

Fillings and Sauces

Apple Apricot Butter

1 to 2 lbs. golden delicious or greening apples
2 to 3 handfuls dried apricots
water
1 or 2 pinches sea salt

Wash, peel and core apples. Cut in small pieces and place in a large pot with apricots. Add just enough water to cover the bottom of the pan to a depth of about ¼ inch. Add salt and bring to a boil. Reduce heat and simmer, covered, for several hours or until mixture has cooked down to a puree and is darker and sweet.

Serving suggestions:

– This is very concentrated. Serve in very small dishes with a few ground roasted nuts as a topping.

– Use as a topping for a grain-based dessert.

– Serve with very plain cookies or mochi puffs.

– Use as a spread or filling.

Azuki Raisin Puree

1½ cups azuki beans, soaked overnight and drained
3 cups apple juice
3 cups water
5-inch piece kombu
¾ cup raisins
½ tsp. sea salt

Pressure cook beans with apple juice, water, and kombu for 35 to 40 minutes. Remove kombu strip and set aside. Add raisins and salt to azuki beans. Simmer, covered, over low heat for 20 minutes, being careful not to let it burn.

Let mixture cool, then puree in a hand food mill or a sieve. Chill and serve as a pudding or as a filling for baked mochi puffs, azuki bean brownies, or as a pastry filling. Or cool and serve at room temperature.

Very Berry Topping

10-oz. jar fruit juice-sweetened jam (red raspberry, strawberry, blueberry, blackberry, or apricot)
1½ to 2 cups water
2 Tbsp. kuzu or arrowroot

Mix jam with water. Dissolve kuzu or arrowroot in a small amount of cold water. Blend ingredients and bring to a boil, then reduce heat to medium and stir continuously until thickened. Reduce heat as needed, and add more water to prevent burning. Add apple juice or rice syrup if a sweeter taste is desired.

Pour over tofu cheesecake or over vanilla cake, coffee cake, or carob cake.

Chestnut Puree

A deliciously sweet sauce to pour over baked butternut, buttercup, or kabocha squash; baked pears or apples.

≡ 2 heaping cups dried chestnuts
≡ 4 cups water

Soak dried chestnuts in water overnight. Pressure cook chestnuts in the soaking liquid for 30 to 40 minutes. Turn off heat and let mixture sit in the pressure cooker with the lid on for 20 minutes. Then puree in the blender until smooth. Serve warm or at room temperature, or chill until needed.

Maltose

≡ 2 cups sweet brown rice
≡ 1½ cups short grain brown rice
≡ 6 to 8 cups water
≡ ½ cup wheat sprouts
≡ sea salt

Pressure cook rices with water for about 1 hour. The longer you cook it, the sweeter it gets. Use a flame tamer and low heat to avoid scorching. Remove from heat and allow to cool until you can put your finger in and count to ten.

In blender, grind wheat sprouts and a small amount of water. Add to cooled rice. Let mixture sit in a glass or ceramic container 48 hours at the lowest setting of your stove or in a crock pot (not over 135°F). Keep it covered with a glass lid (not metal); stir it occasionally.

After 48 hours blend rice in a blender, then cook over low heat with a few pinches salt. The cooking stops fermentation.

Cook it uncovered if you want excess liquid to evaporate. Mixture will resemble a creamy, thick pudding.

Store in jars and refrigerate.

Serving Suggestions:

– Serve maltose as a pudding.

– Dilute and drink maltose hot or cold with freshly squeezed ginger juice.

– Make a zestier pudding: Thicken with kuzu, add tangerine juice or lemon juice, and sprinkle toasted ground almonds on top.

Raisin Syrup

1 cup raisins
3 cups water

Soak fruit in water for 30 minutes. Bring to a boil, then simmer for 15 minutes. Add more water if necessary. Puree in blender, adding more water if mixture is too thick. Serve warm or cold on toast, hot cereal, pancakes, or waffles. Refrigerate; it keeps 1 to 2 weeks.

Variation:

– Use dried apricots in place of raisins.

Raisin Sauce

3 cups raisins
6 cups water
4 Tbsp. agar agar flakes
1 cup water

Soak raisins in 6 cups water 1 to 2 hours. Boil, then simmer 15 minutes. Soak agar agar in 1 cup water. Add agar agar and water to raisins and bring to a boil again, then simmer 8 to 10 minutes. Blenderize until smooth. Refrigerate in glass jars.

Serving Suggestions:

– Spoon over waffles, pancakes, or whole wheat French toast.

– Pour over a cake or other dessert.

– Spoon over toast with sesame or almond butter.

Squash Cream

Scrub 3 to 4 organic delicatta, kabocha, Hokkaido, or sweet dumpling squash. Cut in half, then fourths. Remove seeds and pulp, then cut squash into 2-inch pieces. Leave skin on if desired. Skin can be eaten if it is organic, soft, and not too woody. Boil in a pot with 2 to 3 inches of water for 30 minutes or until squash is soft. Or pressure cook 15 minutes and let squash sit in the pot 15 minutes. Puree in a food mill or blender. Add cinnamon or other sweet spices, if desired. Add more water to thin, if necessary. Spoon over desserts or on pancakes and waffles.

Variations:

– Squash Puree with Spices and Nuts

> For 6 cups pureed squash, add:
> ½ to 1 tsp. cinnamon
> ¼ tsp. nutmeg
> ½ cup chopped and roasted walnuts (use as garnish, if desired)
> ½ cup chopped and roasted pumpkin seeds (optional).

– Amasake and Squash Cream

> For 4 cups pureed squash, add:
> ½ to 1 cup amasake rice nectar or amasake almond rice nectar.

Tofu Whipped Cream

2 lbs. tofu
6-oz. package plain soy drink
grated rind of 1 lemon
6 Tbsp. rice malt

Steam tofu for 10 to 15 minutes. Blenderize or whip with soy drink, lemon rind, and rice malt until mixture is creamy.

Chill and serve over Quick Apple Crisp, baked apples or pears, or fruit kantens.

Variations:

– Substitute carob, vanilla, mocha, or other flavored soy drink.

Tofu Maple Whipped Cream

2 lbs. tofu
¼ to ⅓ cup sesame tahini
¼ to ⅓ cup maple syrup
3 Tbsp. lemon juice
½ to ¼ cups water

Steam tofu for 10 to 15 minutes. Blenderize or whip with other ingredients, adding them according to taste and adding water a little at a time to make a creamy and fluffy consistency.

Vanilla Sauce

½ cup sesame butter
1 Tbsp. water
½ cup sweet rice flour
⅛ tsp. sea salt
1 vanilla bean, split lengthwise or 1 tsp. vanilla
3 cups apple juice

Heat sesame butter with water over low heat; add flour. Saute for a few minutes, then remove from heat. Add salt, vanilla, and apple juice. Simmer uncovered for 30 minutes, stirring occasionally. Add water if it becomes too thick. Remove vanilla bean and serve warm or chill and whip for a lighter consistency.

Serving Suggestions:

– Serve over baked apples or pears, or gingerbread cake, or apple pie.

Mim Collins-Drewry

Frostings

Amasake Frosting

8.8-oz. package or 1 cup plus 2 Tbsp. amasake
¾ cup water
1 Tbsp. kuzu or arrowroot
vanilla or almond extract
grated lemon or orange rind
1 cup almonds or walnuts, roasted and chopped

Mix amasake with ½ cup water. Mix remaining water with
kuzu or arrowroot, stirring until it is dissolved. Combine
amasake and kuzu, and heat over medium heat 3 to 4 minutes, stirring, until thickened. Add vanilla or almond extract
and citrus rind.

Mix in nuts; chill until mixture is cool. Frost between
layers and on top of Couscous Layer Cake.

Tip:

– Use more or less water depending on consistency of amasake.

Rice Malt Kuzu Glaze

For mochi croutons, cakes, pies, couscous balls, etc.

- 1 heaping Tbsp. kuzu
- 1 cup cold water
- 1 cup plus 2 to 3 Tbsp. rice syrup

Place kuzu in water and dissolve lumps, using a suribachi if desired. Place in saucepan, then add rice syrup and bring mixture to a boil. Simmer over low heat 3 to 5 minutes, stirring well and being careful not to burn the bottom. Remove from heat and continue to stir. It will thicken as it cools. Spoon over couscous balls, porridge, rice puddings, cakes, baked mochi croutons, or other desserts. Save leftover rice malt kuzu glaze in a jar in the refrigerator.

Tofu Cream Frosting

- 1 lb. tofu
- 2 to 3 Tbsp. tahini
- 1 to 2 tsp. vanilla
- ⅔ cup rice syrup or maple syrup
- 1 pinch sea salt
- 2 to 3 tsp. lemon juice

Steam tofu 5 to 10 minutes. Mix all ingredients in a blender. Chill; frost cake just before serving. Makes enough for two 9-inch cakes.

To decorate, make a ring of chopped, roasted walnuts or almonds around edge of cake.

Chestnut Cream Frosting

≡ 1 cup dried chestnuts
2½ cups water

Soak dried chestnuts in water overnight. Add apple juice or water if necessary so chestnuts are covered, and pressure cook chestnuts in their soak water for 45 minutes.

Blenderize chestnuts and their liquid while they are still hot. If you want a thinner consistency, thin with warm apple juice. If you blend or cream the chestnuts when they get cold, it will be almost impossible to get a creamy consistency because of their high fat content.

Carob Chestnut Cream Frosting

≡ 1 cup hot Chestnut Cream Frosting
½ to 1 cup or less tahini, sesame butter, or almond butter
2 Tbsp. carob powder
1 tsp. orange rind or lemon rind, grated
¼ tsp. sea salt
1 tsp. vanilla
1 tsp. cinnamon (optional)
hot apple juice to blend

Blenderize hot chestnut cream frosting, tahini, and carob. Add rind, sea salt, vanilla, and cinnamon. Keep blending until desired consistency is reached. (The longer you blend, the thicker it becomes.) Use hot apple juice to adjust the consistency.

Serving suggestions:

– Frost cake and sprinkle grated coconut or toasted coconut flakes on top for a snowy effect.

– This frosting is great on a carob cake.

Pecan Malt Glaze

½ cup water
½ cup rice syrup and/or barley malt syrup
2 Tbsp. agar agar
¼ tsp. cinnamon
⅛ tsp. salt
½ cup pecan or walnut halves, toasted
⅓ tsp. vanilla extract

Mix water, syrup, agar agar, cinnamon, and salt. Bring mixture to a boil, then simmer, stirring occasionally, until agar agar is completely dissolved (about 5 minutes). Let mixture cool 15 minutes, then add vanilla and pecans or walnuts and pour glaze on top of Couscous Layer Cake. Optional: place the nuts on top of the cake, then pour on glaze. Let cake sit until glaze is hardened.

The cake will keep at room temperature for a day or so. Cover and refrigerate, if desired.

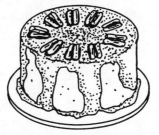

Maple Tofu Cream Frosting

A creamy white frosting for cakes, cupcakes, and carob brownies.

1 lb. soft tofu
½ to ⅔ cup maple syrup
1 tsp. vanilla
pinch sea salt
3 Tbsp. fresh lemon juice (optional)
1 Tbsp. safflower oil or 2 Tbsp. tahini

Steam tofu 5 to 10 minutes, then blenderize with other ingredients, adding water as needed to allow smooth blending. Frosting should be thick and creamy. It can be made ahead and chilled. Frost cake right before serving, then refrigerate leftover iced cake.

Serving Suggestions and Variations:

– After frosting cake,
- sprinkle carob chips in a circle around outside of cake;
- make a ring of roasted almonds or walnuts around outer edges of cake; or
- sprinkle with carob powder or coconut flakes.

– For Carob Cream Frosting, add 3 heaping tablespoons carob powder and omit the lemon juice.

– Use rice syrup in place of maple syrup.

Mocha Whip Frosting

12 oz. tofu, boiled 10 minutes and drained
6 Tbsp. rice syrup or maple syrup, or to taste
½ tsp. vanilla
3 Tbsp grain coffee powder
3 Tbsp. carob powder

Blenderize ingredients. Spread on cake and sprinkle with a
bit of grain coffee powder, unsweetened coconut, or grated
lemon rind.

Miscellany

☰ *How to Start Your Day*

Whether you have your first meal at 6:00 a.m. or at 8:00 or 9:00 a.m., breakfast is an important meal. Taking in the bulk of your food early in the day when you are most active is better than having a big meal and sleeping on it. Most macrobiotic eaters know the value of not eating within three hours of going to bed.

Many people who say they aren't hungry in the morning have eaten late dinners or snacked late at night. You may be amazed to find that if you get in the habit of eating dinner at 5:00 or 6:00 and not snacking or eating after 6:30 or 7:00 p.m., it is much easier to get a restful sleep and get up early. And yes, you will be hungry in the morning.

I find that breakfast really fuels me and when I go without it – or without a substantial brunch or lunch meal – I tend to snack or eat more later in the day. Sometimes I just have a larger brunch meal at 11:00 a.m. rather than fussing with two smaller meals.

There are no limitations to the morning meal.

Soup: Sweet pumpkin, onion, parsnip, rutabaga, carrot, turnip, or azuki beans and vegetable soup with miso, or other combinations serve well first thing in the morning – especially if left over from the day or night before, when the vegetables become sweeter after the miso blends with the vegetables.

Cereal: Hot oatmeal, cream of wheat, cream of buckwheat, whole cooked wheat berries, rice cream, whole cooked oat groats, whole soft cooked rice, leftover rice, millet, or other grain cooked until soft with more water; dry cereals such as brown rice crispy cereal, oatios, granola made without oil, sugars, honey or preservatives.

Cereal Toppers: Sprinkle shiso leaf condiment, gomashio, or other roasted seeds on hot cereal or cook an umeboshi plum in your cereal grains instead of a pinch of two of sea salt. Chopped roasted almonds and raisins or applesauce or apple butter are good in or on oats or oat porridge. A dash of amasake concentrate gives a sweet, creamy taste. For a milky flavor you can use diluted amasake or prepare oat milk, almond milk, or other nut milks by soaking nuts overnight, blanching them with boiling water, and blenderizing them. Soy milk is okay occasionally, but it is a processed food, not a whole food.

Side Dishes with Hot Cereals or Grains: Soft cooked cauliflower with diluted umeboshi vinegar, leftover carrot matchsticks, pumpkin butter, onion butter, soft cooked Brussels sprouts with a dash of umeboshi vinegar or rice vinegar diluted in water, or leftover delicatta, buttercup, or Hokkaido squash chunks. Crispy steamed greens cooked with a pinch of sea salt. Light pickles – a nice complement to a bowl of leftover porridge.

Breads: Naturally-leavened breads and unleavened pita bread or whole wheat chapatis or pancakes are better than yeasted breads which are more mucus-forming, gas producing and less digestible; check labels for additives, sugar, honey, oil, and yeast.

Spreads: Almond butter, toasted sesame butter or other nut butters can be spread on bread or pancakes. Unsweetened apple butter, apple-apricot, apple-strawberry, and other pure fruit butters can be spread on toast or cereal. Whole grain breads are good with mustard, sesame butter, and sauerkraut with or without chopped scallions. Tofu cheese is good on bread or crackers with sprouts, scallions, or blanched greens.

Other Breakfast Ideas:

– Rice balls made with pressure-cooked brown rice, toasted nori seaweed, umeboshi plum.

– Pan-fried rice with scallions, vegies, a dash of shoyu and ginger juice.

– Scrambled tofu, rice or udon noodles, steamed broccoli or carrots and parsley.

– Pureed azuki beans and squash made into soup, served with rice, rice balls, or mochi.

– Sweet pumpkin or squash soup with soft rice, soft millet, or oatmeal on the side.

– Pan-fried millet loaf slices with a dash of shoyu and wrapped in nori strips.

– Pan-fried polenta slices with shoyu and wrapped in large shiso leaf strips and nori.

– Daikon, onion, wakame miso soup with mochi puffs or rice.

– Leftover baked or steamed squash, leftover greens, rice sprinkled with gomashio.

– Rice cakes, tofu spread, blanched or steamed kale, carrot, broccoli or leeks, scallion.

– Rice cakes with thin layer of tahini or sesame butter, mustard, minced scallion, sauerkraut.

– Bancha tea, roasted barley tea, grain coffee, roasted corn tea, roasted dandelion tea, or other macrobiotic grain beverage to accompany your meal, if desired.

Use your imagination and creativity to find what works for you.

☰ *Pack Lunch Ideas*

You can make sandwiches with various bean spreads, seitan (wheat meat), tempeh, or tofu and fresh or cooked vegetables. If you want bread for your sandwich, it is best to use whole grain unyeasted natural-rise breads and flat breads like whole wheat pita bread, tortillas, or chapatis. (Yeast may cause bloating, gas, excess stomach acid, and can prevent absorption of some vitamins and minerals in the food.) Alfalfa or mung bean sprouts are good on sandwiches or in salads with chopped lettuce, radishes, carrots or some other vegetables. Occasionally include pressed salad or homemade pickles.

– Whole wheat pita bread or chapatis stuffed with Chickpea Spread and alfalfa sprouts.

– Pack rice cakes or rice crackers along with a container filled with Chickpea Spread and some sauteed chopped leeks or raw chopped scallions for a garnish.

– Split Pea Cashew Pate or Lentil Pate with bread, rice cakes, or crackers.

– Tofu Sour Cream, cooked vegetables, and crackers or rice cakes.

– Bean burgers or loaves.

– Tempeh and sauerkraut sandwich on lightly toasted whole wheat bread, pita bread, or chapatis.

– Tempeh sauteed with fresh mushrooms and served with steamed greens or rolled in blanched cabbage leaves after mixing with rice and/or lightly cooked or sauteed vegetables.

– Pureed squash, parsnip, onion spread: nishime vegetables, mashed or pureed with roasted tahini or sesame butter diluted with water plus a sprinkle of shoyu.

– Seitan sandwiches: cooked seitan, mustard and sauerkraut in whole wheat pita bread.

– Leftover casseroles can be wrapped and packed.

≡ *Creative Leftovers*

One need never throw away leftovers. In fact, leftovers may be as good as or better than the meals from which they originated.

Oftentimes, foods left unrefrigerated overnight take on a sweeter, richer taste when left to sit in the juices or marinades in which they were cooked. Beans, however, because of their fat content are best refrigerated to prevent rancidity. Leftover vegetables which have been seasoned with a pinch of sea salt, shoyu, or miso during cooking will keep unrefrigerated for a day or so; soups seasoned with miso or shoyu will become extraordinarily sweet if they contain root vegetables such as turnip, carrot, onion, or squash which seem to combine with the salt in the miso to add richness. Cooked grains keep longer than cooked land or sea vegetables, soups, or beans. They will last for at least three days when kept at cool room temperature. Often a few umeboshi plum pits or sections stuck in rice keep it fresher. Store in a glass, wooden, or ceramic bowl, and cover rice with a bamboo sushi mat to allow it to breathe. Refrigeration can change the quality and flavor of the food. Freezing is usually not recommended in macrobiotic cooking.

Leftover soup may taste better when reheated before serving. Grain doesn't need reheating unless it has become dry and you want to steam or pan-fry it. Most leftover vegetable dishes can be eaten as is, or sauteed with rice, made into a pate with beans, or put into soup. Remember that the vegetables have already gone through a cooking and seasoning process, so cooking and salting them again is rather unnecessary.

Keep it simple, and remember the mark of a good cook is not the ability to use elaborate techniques and exotic spices which may mask the true flavor of the ingredients. Rather, a good cook is one who knows how to bring out the subtle flavors with the least amount of interference.

Grains:

– Cook 1 part cooked grain with 3 to 4 parts water to make a soft porridge, or add more water and cook with finely cut vegetables to make a grain stew. It can be seasoned with miso, shoyu, umeboshi plum or pits.

– Grain burgers: Mix cooked rice, barley, wheat berries, or some combination of cooked grains with cooked lentils and chopped roasted walnuts or sunflower seeds, grated carrots, celery, onion, or scallions. Season with miso, shoyu, or umeboshi paste. Form into burgers or loaves and grill or bake until golden brown; or roll into balls and deep-fry. Try millet and cauliflower burgers with Walnut Miso Gravy. Experiment with any combination of grains and nuts, grains and beans, or grains and beans and vegetables.

– Nori rolls: Flatten cooked rice onto sheets of toasted nori seaweed, place a thin row of cooked vegetable strips, pickles, or pickles and nut butter on the rice, then roll into logs and cut with a wet knife as for Sushi.

– Rice-crust pizza: Moisten and flatten cooked rice onto a lightly oiled cookie sheet or pizza pan. Top with cooked tempeh, crumbled tofu, azuki bean, lentil or chickpea puree, chopped onion, scallions, shoyu-cooked mushrooms, grated carrot, alfalfa sprouts, or steamed broccoli or cauliflower. Grate dried mochi on top of the pizza and bake; it will bubble and turn crispy as it melts into the pizza like mozzarella cheese.

– Casseroles: Almost any leftover grains, beans, nuts or seeds, minced vegetables and condiments can be made into a loaf or casserole. See Pumpkin Tofu Noodle Casserole and Millet Mound.

– Grain balls: Mix leftover cooked grains (rice, millet, etc.) with ground nuts or seeds. Add blanched or raw shredded vegetables if desired. Lightly bake until warm or crisp. Serve with a bechamel sauce, Walnut Miso Gravy, or Tofu Sauce.

– Baked goods and desserts: Leftover oatmeal or other cooked cereals can be used to make cookies, biscuits, or breads. Adding raisins, juice, grated apples, or other dried fruits and nuts or seeds can transform leftover cereal into a marvelous dessert. Rice, raisins, and rice syrup or barley malt make a wonderful rice pudding when baked in the oven or cooked on the stove. Roasted nuts, seeds, or nut butter or soy milk can be cooked in as well. These are occasional treats and not suggested for daily use, as they can be quite rich.

Beans:

– Pate: Put leftover beans in a pot with cooked vegetables. Cover with water and bring to a boil, then reduce heat and simmer until beans are soft and creamy. Add fresh parsley or scallions at the end. Good combinations are:

- azuki beans with carrots, onions or squash, shoyu, ginger and scallions;
- lentils, onions, wakame, miso, and chopped scallions;

     - split peas, wakame, cauliflower, onions, miso, and
       chopped parsley;

     - chickpeas, carrot, onion, light miso, and scallions or
       parsley.

Use in sandwiches or on rice cakes or crackers.

– Soups: Add more water to the above combinations, adjust-
ing seasonings to taste.

– Burgers, Rissoles: Mix left over beans with nuts, seeds,
leftover cooked grains, and vegetables or condiments.
Tofu burgers can be made by mashing raw or steamed
tofu with grains and forming into burgers and baking,
grilling, or frying.

– Non-meat loaf: This is popular with guests, as are lentil
and walnut meatballs. See Lentil Non-Meat Loaf for ideas.

– Aspics: Mix cooked beans with agar agar, water, and vegetables; cook and allow to set. Good combinations are:

     - lentil and celery; or lentil, celery, and walnut;
     - azukis and raisins;
     - split peas and onion.

Vegetables:

– Spruce up steamed vegetables with rice vinegar or a dressing of rice vinegar, shoyu, and water the day they are
cooked, which will leave them slightly pickled for the next
day.

– Butters: Puree nishime-cooked vegetables with toasted
ground sesame seed plus umeboshi paste if the vegetables
need seasoning. Use pumpkin, carrot, onion, parsnip, or a
mixture of these vegetables.

– Hors d'oeuvres: Roll cooked vegetables in toasted sesame

seeds or crumbled nori.

– Aspics: Mix cooked, pureed vegetables with water and agar agar. Cook and allow to set to make a gelled entree.

– Soups: Leftover vegetable tops, ends, cores, and stalks or stems make wonderful soup stock. Cook them for 30 to 60 minutes in water, then discard vegetable scraps. Save the water and add onions and other fresh vegetables, miso or shoyu, and a garnish.

Seaweeds:

– Seaweeds can be put into vegetable or bean soups with miso or root vegetables. They can be added to boiled or blanched vegetable salads, grain salads, or bean salads.

– Saute leftover arame with toasted seeds or nuts and scallions, with or without rice.

– Save leftover kombu and add to the bottom of a pot of beans or nishime-cooked vegetables. Kombu cuts down on cooking time, makes beans more digestible, and adds minerals to the foods with which it is cooked.

– Toasted nori can be added to soups as a condiment or garnish.

☰ *Cooking for Cravings*

Cravings can be a wonderful opportunity to get in touch with our bodies and to experiment with our cooking. Often we forget that macrobiotics means living in accord with our environment. That means changing our diet as our bodies change, as our condition changes, and as our lifestyles or environments change.

Tune in to what is craved: sweet, sour, bitter, salty, creamy, crunchy, etc. Try to satisfy the craving with clean macrobiotic foods rather than foods you formerly ate which can set off a series of destructive chain reactions and get in the way of healing, cleansing, and moving forward in your life. Learn to let go of the past and learn to deal with things differently.

– Remember what you have eaten in the last few days for a clue to cravings. Lots of baked food, fish, shoyu or salt, any amount of eggs or animal foods – even an overdose of rice can set off a craving for sweets.

– Consider your activity over the last few days or weeks. A stressful situation, tension, and anxiety can make you reach for a sweet or treat to unwind, relax, or phase out.

– Try to add more richness to your daily cooking if you find you are bingeing frequently. Maybe you just need more variety or creative inspiration from friends.

– Learn what cravings mean. Are you eating too rigidly, eating unbalanced meals, relying too heavily on condiments? Are you in a rut, or just discharging old foods? Often we crave what we are discharging and must just be patient and find a healthy substitute.

What to Eat for Specific Cravings:

Bitter: Grain coffee, burdock, dandelion, roasted seeds, chicory, endive. Steamed greens such as kale or collards can be bitter.

Bread: Use brown rice noodles, udon noodles, or other whole wheat noodles which are more digestible than baked flour products. Experiment with millet to make nut loaves or millet and bean bread.

Cheese: Tofu Cheese; Cauliflower "Cheese" Bake; Tofu Sour Cream; Scrambled Tofu Cheese; pureed chickpeas with tahini or sesame butter and white miso; chickpeas with onion, miso, and kuzu; beans pureed and used on crackers, in sauces or burgers.

Crunch: Rice cakes top the list but watch what you put on them. Use tahini and nut butters in moderation. Hot air popcorn sprayed with a mixture of shoyu and water or umeboshi vinegar and water can be very tasty. Popcorn, crumbled rice cakes, or brown rice crispy cereal can be made into Rice Malt Crunch Balls.

Meat: Try lentil nut roasts if it is the meaty oiliness you crave. Lentils with walnuts and miso are quite satisfying. Try tempeh marinated and grilled like steak or as a pate with mushrooms, onion, and shoyu. Seitan is a winner in generously seasoned vegetable stews, stuffed, sauteed, or in a mustard and sauerkraut sandwich (using sourdough whole wheat or rye bread). Walnut Miso Gravy over Millet Mound gives a meaty taste when dark miso is used.

Salt: Miso, shoyu, umeboshi. Use sparingly. Gomashio can be helpful and gives crunchy, salty, and oily tastes all in one. These condiments also bring out the sweetness in cooked vegetables, soups and stews. Remember to season your foods with salt, shoyu, or miso in your cooking, not at the table, where they will send you to the barley malt jar or the health food store for rice ice cream.

Sour: Lemon, umeboshi, sauerkraut, or rice vinegar can satisfy this craving. Often when we crave sweet, we can use sour instead. Try rice vinegar on boiled salads, or umeboshi paste on soft cooked Brussels sprouts and turnips, or lemon rind pressure-cooked with rice.

Sweet: Use acorn, buttercup, delicatta, or kabocha squash baked or nishime cooked; nishime-cooked carrots, onions, or parsnips; Onion Butter; whole onion miso soup or whole cooked onion; Onion Mochi Bake, or mochi with grain sweeteners such as rice malt or barley malt. Sweet fermented grains, such as Amasake, are good for desserts. Use fruit in small amounts and if you live in a temperate climate, choose a temperate-climate fruit like apple instead of tropical varieties like dates or bananas.

How to Care for Your Cast Iron

To season a new cast iron pan, wash with warm water and mild soap, then dry. Pour 2 tablespoons refined vegetable oil into pan, rotating it so the oil coats the bottom and sides evenly. Do not use unrefined oils to season cast iron as they will leave a sticky film on the surface. Place pan in a 225°F oven for 3 hours, then turn off and let it sit overnight. Wipe off excess oil.

When using your cast iron pan, remove food as soon as it is cooked. Rinse pan with hot water, using a mild soap only if necessary. Never use liquid detergent on cast iron as it will remove the finish. Wipe the pan with a sponge and dry immediately on the stove or in the oven. If you have cooked in oil, wipe the pan clean instead of washing. Avoid cooking acidic food (tomatoes, apples, vinegar) in cast iron.

If your cast iron rusts, rub the rust spots with steel wool until the surface feels smooth. Rinse with warm water and mild soap and follow the directions for seasoning a new pan.

≣ *Salt in Foods*

Salt is a natural element in the body and is essential for the body to function. Cellular processes depend on the potassium/sodium balance to maintain life and cellular respiration and repair.

Although miso, shoyu, tamari, pickles, and sea salt are used in a macrobiotic diet, the diet as a whole is lower in sodium than the standard American diet. Miso, tamari, and sea salt are used in small amounts, and only in cooking; they are generally not added at the table. By adding them during cooking you create a more balanced dish and bring out the natural flavors in the food.

Naturally-aged miso and shoyu or tamari provide beneficial enzymes, help balance the acidity of foods, bring out the flavor, and help prevent gas. Commercial soy sauce does not provide the same minerals, enzymes, and properties of naturally-aged shoyu, as it is made very quickly and often contains corn syrup, artificial coloring, and other chemicals to produce a dark, palatable liquid.

Salt in its raw form should not be added at the table, as this overworks the kidneys and causes thirst. It may also prompt a craving for sweets and an excessive appetite.

The Calcium Controversy
by Jorge Badillo-Cochran, N.D.*

In our society, we have been brainwashed to believe that the best and only sources of calcium are dairy products. When it is recommended that dairy products be avoided, the most common question is, "Where do I get my calcium?" The next few pages will show you the facts about calcium and provide a better knowledge of its absorption or non-absorption in the body.

1. The ratio of calcium to phosphorus in the body must be close to 1:1. The average North American diet is between 1:2 and 1:4. The excess phosphorus in the body causes negative calcium balance, meaning that the body eliminates more calcium than it absorbs. Foods high in phosphorus are meats, soft drinks, and some food additives.

2. Excess simple sugars — sucrose and fructose (white sugar, brown sugar, molasses, processed foods, concentrated fruit sweeteners, honey) — will also alter the calcium/phosphorus ratio. Excess simple sugars (especially the more refined ones) "rob" the body of minerals in order to be assimilated.

3. Excess protein in the diet, especially from animal sources including dairy, also causes negative calcium balance due to the high phosphorus and high fat content. Researchers from the University of Wisconsin found that people who consume 102 grams of protein (very common) excreted twice as much

calcium as those who consume the Recommended Dietary Allowance (RDA) of 44 grams. The RDA is easily met in a vegetarian diet.

4. A vegetarian diet (both lacto-ovo and vegan) has been associated with a lower incidence of osteoporosis (American Journal of Clinical Nutrition, #37:453-6, 1983).

5. Milk and milk products contain an unbalanced ratio of calcium to phosphorus and are high in fat. Vitamin D is added to milk to increase the absorption of the calcium; however, it has been found that the calcium is deposited in the joints and soft tissues of the body, which causes more problems. In England, it is against the law to add Vitamin D to milk!

6. Foods from the nightshade family — potatoes, tomatoes, eggplant, red and green peppers, tobacco — have been found to promote calcification of the joints and body tissues. Smoking, in particular, affects calcium balance and overall health.

7. Foods high in acidity, such as alcohol, some vinegars, and citrus require "buffers" such as calcium in order to be assimilated. Several studies have shown that alcohol consumption interferes with the absorption of calcium and can be toxic to bone cells.

8. Oxalic acid (found in spinach, chard, beet greens, parsley, unhulled sesame seeds) binds calcium and makes it more difficult to assimilate.

9. Caffeine (coffee, chocolate, colas and other soft drinks, black tea) blocks the absorption of calcium.

10. Aluminum (cookware, most baking powders, antacids) increases urinary and fecal excretion of unabsorbed calcium.

Now that you know some of the facts, you can see why there is such concern about getting enough calcium — most of the calcium taken in the average North American diet goes unabsorbed. So, it's not how much calcium you take in, but how much is usable. The minimum calcium needed, determined by experiment, is 150 to 200 milligrams per day (mg/day). Worldwide, calcium intake in most populations is 300 to 500 mg/day; the Food and Nutrition Board for the United States recommends 800 mg/day; and recently the National Institute of Health for the United States recommended 1200 to 1500 mg/day. It's very confusing to see so much discrepancy! Why such a large difference? It's all a matter of lifestyle and diet (and of absorption).

Exercise has been found to increase bone mass. Moderate exercise, for one hour three times a week, or 20 minutes a day, is most beneficial. Lack of exercise doubles the rate of urinary and fecal calcium excretion!

* Jorge Badillo-Cochran is a naturopathic doctor who practices in Bellevue, Washington. Reprinted with permission.

Non-Dairy Sources of Calcium
(easily absorbable)

	Amount	Milligrams
Agar agar	3.5 oz.	400
Sardines, with bones	3.0 oz.	372
Mustard greens	1 cup	285
Turnip greens	1 cup	252
Bok choy	1 cup	250
Collard greens	1 cup	220
Kale	1 cup	200
Broccoli	1 cup	160
Hijiki, cooked	¼ cup	152
Sesame tahini	2 Tbsp.	132
Wakame, cooked	¼ cup	130
Tempeh	3.0 oz.	129
Tofu	3.5 oz.	120
Watercress	½ cup	090
Kombu, cooked	¼ cup	076
Sauerkraut	⅔ cup	045

Other sources: beans, nuts, seeds, miso, vegetables.

≣ *Glossary*

Agar agar (also called Kanten) – A natural vegetable gelatin obtained from several varieties of red seaweed that contains no calories and comes in flakes, bars, or powders. Agar agar is used to make gelled desserts with fruit juice or in jams, jellies, puddings, pie fillings, and aspics.

Amasake (also spelled Amazake) – A fermented grain pudding that is often used as a sweetener in cookies, cakes, or frostings. It is also sold as a drink in many natural foods stores. It lends itself to pancake mixes, cakes, or as a cereal topper. The amasake recipes in this book generally make a thick dessert pudding or sweetener for baking.

Arame – A shredded dark brown sea vegetable. It has a milder taste and aroma than its cousin hijiki. Arame is high in protein, vitamins A and B-complex, and all the minerals, particularly calcium, iodine and iron. It is delicious sauteed with vegetables and shoyu or ume vinegar, or boiled with ume vinegar or shoyu with roasted nuts or seeds sprinkled on it.

Azuki beans (also spelled Adzuki and Aduki) – Small, shiny, red beans that are highly regarded for their nutritional and healing properties. They are a good source of protein, vitamins, and minerals. Azuki beans are often cooked with squash and kombu to help restore and maintain proper blood sugar balance. Also good in soups and baked with miso, barley malt, and ginger.

Bancha tea – A macrobiotic staple. Bancha tea includes the leaves and twigs of the tea plant, and it is often interchanged with kuki-cha tea. You can reuse this tea, straining it each time. Cook your brown rice in leftover bancha tea for a nice flavor and color.

Barley malt – A dark, rich syrup made from whole barley that has been sprouted, roasted, and extracted to liquid form. It is less dense and less sweet than honey, and it is absorbed fairly slowly by the body so it is less likely to adversely affect the blood sugar level. It resembles molasses in color and texture but has a somewhat heartier, robust flavor. It is 65 percent maltose.

Brown rice vinegar – A naturally brewed vinegar made from brown rice. It has none of the sharpness or "bite" often found in other vinegars. Use it in salads, dressings, or tofu spreads, or drizzle it on cooked greens. Not all rice vinegars are alike. Many of those found in natural foods stores, Asian markets, or other grocery stores contain sugar and often are of low quality. High quality brown rice vinegars contain a significantly higher amino acid ratio and are thought to help alkalinize the blood and counteract lactic acid buildup caused by strenuous exercise.

Buckwheat – The seeds of an herb, not really a grain. There is no wheat in it. It is very warming and strengthening — a good, hearty winter food. It is sold as groats, grits, or flour. Buckwheat is high in B-complex vitamins, calcium, phosphorus, and protein.

Bulgur – Cooked and dried wheat which has been cracked.

Burdock root – A brownish, slender root popularized by the Japanese, who call it gobo. It is always served cooked and has an earthy aroma and flavor. Medicinally, it is said to be a blood purifier and strengthening to the kidneys.

Carob – A powder ground from roasted carob pods, a popular chocolate substitute. It is nearly 50 percent sugar and 8 percent protein; it is significantly lower in calories and fat than chocolate. It contains none of the caffeine or oxalic acid found in chocolate, and it is naturally sweet. Carob powder is the preferred form to use as carob candies and chips often contain high amounts of saturated fats and sweeteners. Use carob sparingly.

Chestnuts, dried – Large bean-like nuts that have been dried. They are sweet and flavorful and must be soaked in water and cooked for several hours or pressure cooked before using. Do not throw away the soak water, as it is very sweet and mineral rich. Puree of cooked dried chestnuts is used in puddings, sauces, and cake frostings. Dried chestnuts can be cooked whole with rice or sweet rice.

Couscous – The endosperm of durum wheat which has been broken or cracked and steamed. It has a light, nutty taste and cooks quickly. It is a refined product but is handy for occasional use to make quick no-bake cakes as well as many Middle Eastern dishes.

Daikon – A long white radish found in many Asian grocery stores, co-ops, and natural food stores. Traditionally, it is grated and served raw with a dash of shoyu. It is thought to aid digestion and help break down fats and oils in fish and fried foods. Daikon is a natural diuretic. It is good boiled, blanched, or steamed and served in cooked vegetable salads, casseroles, and stews. Try it steamed with parsley.

Dulse – A purple leaf sea vegetable that is especially high in iron. It is used in soups, salads, and vegetable dishes. It needs no cooking – just soak and chop it, then add it to a salad or blend it with a light dressing or combinations of umeboshi vinegar and rice vinegar or sauerkraut juice.

Flaxseed binder – As an egg substitute, two tablespoons of flax-seed are ground to a meal in a coffee or spice mill. Six table-spoons of boiling water are poured over the flaxseed meal and after 15 minutes the mixture is whisked with a fork. This amount replaces 2 eggs in cookies, pancakes, or non-meat burgers and loaves.

Food mill – A steel food mill shaped like a saucepan with holes, with a hand crank; used to puree vegetables, grains, or beans for dips, sauces, soups, and puddings.

Ginger juice – The juice squeezed from freshly grated ginger root. It is often added to soups just before serving or used in mari-nades, sauces, or desserts.

Gomashio – A condiment made from roasted, ground sesame seeds and sea salt. Sprinkle it on vegetables, rice, or other grains.

Grain beverage, grain coffee – Roasted grains in powdered form are sold in most natural food stores under many brand names. They can be used in cakes or puddings where a coffee flavor is de-sired.

Hato mugi ("Job's Tears") – Although it resembles barley, it is really the seed of a grass similar to rice. It has twice the protein, iron, vitamin B2, fat, and slightly more calcium than rice. It has a stronger taste than barley or rice and is best cooked in a ratio of 1 part hato mugi to 4 parts short-grain brown rice.

Hato mugi cha – Tea made from roasted hato mugi.

Hijiki – A stringy black sea vegetable that is especially high in calcium. It is usually sauteed with vegetables or tofu. It grows off the coast of Japan.

Kanten – see agar agar.

Kombu – A dark sea vegetable that is sold in thick, long strips. It is used in soups and stews or cooked with beans and tempeh to enhance flavor and aid in digestion. Kombu is high in calcium, iron, iodine, vitamins A and B-complex, plus numerous other trace minerals. It is said to lower cholesterol and relieve water retention.

Kukicha – A tea that contains only the twigs of the tea plant; it is also known as twig tea. The caffeine and tannin content of this tea are very low. Kukicha twigs may be reused by straining the twigs when the tea is served and leaving them in the pot. Serve it hot or cold, with or without lemon or apple juice.

Kuzu – A white starch made from the root of a wild plant called kudzu. It is used to thicken soups, sauces, puddings, and gravies. Kuzu enhances the flavor and adds iron, calcium, and phosphorus. It is sometimes used for medicinal purposes to strengthen digestion and to relieve general fatigue.

Lotus root – A root related to the water lily. It is brown skinned, hollow chambered, and is a beige color inside. Lotus root has a mild flavor and combines well with other vegetables in stir-fried dishes, thinly cut and deep fried or pan fried. It can be pressure cooked with rice or sauteed with arame. Medicinally, it is believed to be beneficial to the respiratory organs.

Lotus seeds – In Oriental medicine, they are eaten to increase energy and vitality and for reproductive disorders. Lotus seeds are sold whole or in split form and require presoaking. They are delicious pressure cooked with short-grain brown rice and hato mugi or lotus root, or cooked with wakame.

Maple syrup – A product of maple sap. It has a lower sucrose

content than sugar but does cause some of the same insulin and
adrenaline reactions produced by sugar. It comes in several
grades; the highest grades have a higher sugar content, while the
lower grades contain more trace minerals. There may be problems
with lead and/or formaldehyde toxicity associated with the col-
lection and production of maple syrup. In most recipes calling for
maple syrup, rice syrup can be substituted.

Millet – Mainly grown for birdseed and cattle feed in North
America, millet is one of the oldest foods known to humans and is
the chief source of carbohydrate for the Northern Chinese and
many people in Africa and India. It is high in B-complex vitamins
and protein, as well as lecithin, calcium, iron, magnesium, phosphorus, and potassium. It lends itself to a variety of uses. Try it
cooked with sweet rice or served with squash, cauliflower or onions, as a porridge, or in a variety of other dishes.

Mirin – A sweet cooking wine made from sweet rice and used in
marinades, sauces, and other dishes. Read the ingredients label,
as not all mirin products are alike.

Miso – A mineral and enzyme-rich paste made from fermented
soybeans and usually a grain such as rice or barley. It is commonly used to season soups, added just before serving so as to retain
the beneficial digestive enzymes that would be lost by boiling.
Miso is also used to flavor gravies, salad dressings, sauces, marinades, dips, and sandwich spreads. It can be mixed with beans
and stews. Miso is available in light and dark forms which vary in
saltiness, sweetness, flavor, and length of fermentation time. Miso
contains protein and B-complex vitamins. Unpasteurized misos
are preferable, as they contain more nutrients than pasteurized
misos.

Mochi – Sweet rice which has been cooked, pounded, and dried,
then cut into cakes or squares. Mochi can be baked, pan fried,

broiled, deep fried, or grated (to make a topping for casseroles, pizzas, or apple crisps). It expands and puffs up when baked or deep fried and resembles a cream puff or a crouton when baked in small pieces. It is strengthening and lends itself to a variety of uses. Mochi is available in several flavors.

Mu tea – A strong-tasting herb tea made from nine ("Mu-9") or sixteen ("Mu-16") herbs. It can be served hot with apple juice, like a spiced cider.

Nori – A sea vegetable that is dried and pressed into thin sheets, commonly used for sushi rolls – wrapped around combinations of rice, vegetables, pickles, or fish. It is high in vitamins A, B, and C, protein, calcium, and iron. Nori is also used to make rice balls and is crumbled into soups, scrambled tofu, or salads.

Nori-maki sushi – Rolled rice generally wrapped in sheets of nori seaweed and filled with pickles, vegetables, and/or fish and sliced into rounds.

Oat groats, whole oats – The whole oat kernels, which are hulled. They are less refined than rolled oats or steel cut oats. They require soaking and lengthy cooking but make a wonderful, creamy porridge. Try 1 part oat groats per 4 to 5 parts water in a crock pot overnight.

Pressure cooker – A pressure-regulated pot with a tight-fitting lid used to cook beans, rice, and other foods. Larger pressure cookers are used for canning. Pressure cooking seals in the nutrients of foods and tends to make them more digestible. Beans are cooked in substantially less time and rendered more digestible than by boiling. Rice takes no less time but tends to be more soft, digestible, and flavorful when cooked in a pressure cooker.

Rice syrup – A smooth, light syrup that looks like honey but is made from sprouted barley mixed with cooked rice, which is then naturally fermented to break down the rice starch into maltose. Maltose is considered superior to sucrose (white sugar) in that it requires no insulin for absorption so it does not upset the blood sugar level the way other sweeteners such as honey, corn syrup, and maple syrup do. Rice syrup's mild flavor works well in pancakes, cookies, cakes, and other desserts.

Roasted barley tea – A tea made by brewing roasted barley. It helps stimulate digestion after a meal. It can be used with apple juice for a hot or cooling beverage.

Sea salt – Sun dried or kiln baked salt which has been obtained from the ocean rather than mined from inland deposits. Unrefined sea salt is high in trace minerals and contains no chemicals, sugar, or added iodine.

Seitan ("wheat meat") – A gluten product that is high in protein and easy to digest. It has the appearance and texture of meat. Use it in soups, stews, casseroles, pates, sandwiches, and stir-fries.

Sesame butter – A sesame spread made from unhulled sesame seeds, sold toasted or raw. It is generally a bit heavier than tahini. Try sesame butter on crackers, bread, or in recipes where a rich, nutty taste is desired.

Shiitake – A mushroom often dried and imported from Japan but also now being harvested in this country and sold fresh. Shiitake mushrooms are used in soups, stews, sauces, gravies, stir-fry dishes, and with noodles. Although they are expensive, shiitake mushrooms are rich in flavor and revered for their medicinal value.

Shiso leaf – Generally used in a dried, powdered form, or found in jars of pickled umeboshi plums. Shiso is also known as beefsteak leaf and gives umeboshi plums their pinkish-red color. Shi-so leaf is high in iron and is known for its medicinal properties. In its powdery, salty form, it makes a nice condiment. Sprinkle it on grains or vegetable dishes, or mix it with roasted ground sesame or pumpkin seeds.

Short-grain brown rice – A staple for most people who follow a macrobiotic diet. It has a nice mild flavor and is easily digested when it is pressure cooked 45 to 50 minutes. It is good as a break-fast porridge or rice cream. It can be used to make desserts such as amasake as well as in making nori-maki sushi.

Shoyu (see also tamari) – A dark liquid made from soybeans and wheat and naturally fermented; naturally-aged soy sauce. Like miso, it contains amino acids, minerals, and some B-complex vita-mins. but it is used primarily for its outstanding taste. It enhances the flavor of marinated vegetables, soups, and especially beans, soups, sautes, pickles, and dressings.

Soy sauce (commercial) – A shoyu- or tamari-like imitation sauce made from hydrolized vegetable protein, caramel coloring, hy-drochloric acid, corn syrup, salt, and water.

Suribachi – A Japanese bowl used for grinding sesame seeds, nuts, gomashio (sesame salt); also handy in mixing sauces and di-luting miso before adding it to soups. It has a ridged, unglazed clay surface, and is used like a mortar with a wooden pestle called a surikogi.

Sushi mat – A bamboo mat used for rolling sushi or to cover con-tainers of cooked rice or leftovers.

Sweet brown rice – A short-grain variety of rice often used in desserts or combined with millet or short-grain brown rice. It is also used to make mochi. It is sweeter and stickier than plain brown rice and contains more protein and slightly more fat than regular rice.

Tahini – A paste made from hulled sesame seeds and sold raw or toasted. It is used in sauces, dressings, cookies and desserts or spread on bread or crackers. Tahini is often mixed with other ingredients for sandwich spreads, bean dips, and casseroles.

Tamari – The salty liquid that is left over and drained from soybean miso after the miso has fermented. Tamari is often considered synonymous with shoyu (naturally-aged soy sauce) but varies in taste and aroma, depending on the length of fermentation. Since it is salty, it is best cooked in food rather than added at the table. A little goes a long way.

Tempeh – A fermented soybean product which is high in protein, and contains B12 and B-complex vitamins. It is a daily staple in Indonesia and is often used as a meat substitute – marinated and fried, or used in casseroles, burgers, stews, etc.

Tofu – A soy "cheese" or bean curd made from soybean milk and sold in block form. Tofu is significantly lower in fat than cheese. It is low in carbohydrate and is 85 percent water. Tofu is an excellent source of calcium and protein. It is easy to digest due to its pre-cooked nature.

Umeboshi paste – A creamy red paste made from umeboshi plums which can be used medicinally or for its sour and salty taste in salad dressings, nori-maki sushi, in tofu or bean dips.

Umeboshi plums – Sour, salt-pickled Japanese plums revered for their medicinal properties. These small red plums contain a number of minerals and organic acids which stimulate digestion and detoxification. The plums are often used medicinally for headaches, motion sickness, food poisoning, and stomach problems.

They are considered a condiment and are not to be used in great quantity.

Umeboshi vinegar – Not really a vinegar in the traditional sense, but the brine from fermented umeboshi plums. It is alkaline, whereas most vinegars are acidic. It is a tart, salty plum vinegar that livens up salad dressings and cooked vegetables. It can be used to make quick pickles or added to tofu spreads and sauces. Due to its salty nature, it is best to dilute it. Try it mixed with brown rice vinegar and oil on vegetable and rice salads.

Wakame – A long, greenish sea vegetable used in soups, salads, and stews. A close relative of alaria, wakame is harvested in Japan and contains calcium and trace minerals.

Wheat berries – The whole wheat kernels, best cooked with rice after presoaking overnight. They can be purchased as soft red winter wheat or hard winter wheat berries. They contain more of the wheat germ, wheat bran, and endosperm than flour and hence are considered a whole food.

Wheat meat – see seitan.

Whole wheat pastry flour – A lighter product than whole wheat flour, best used in cakes and light pastries. It is made from soft wheat berries which contain less gluten than hard wheat.

Yannoh – A caffeine-free grain coffee that contains a mixture of roasted, powdered azuki beans, soybeans, and brown rice. It comes in an instant form and a form for brewing as regular coffee.

Cutting Styles

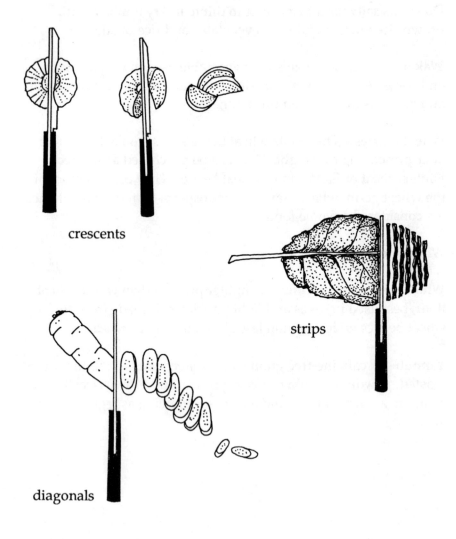

crescents

strips

diagonals

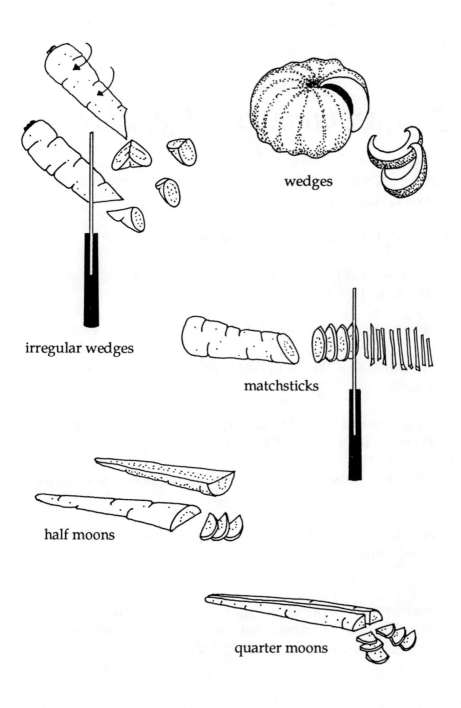

wedges

irregular wedges

matchsticks

half moons

quarter moons

≣ Recommended Reading

Heidenry, Carolyn – *Making the Transition to a Macrobiotic Diet*, Avery, Wayne, 1984.

Kushi, Michio – *The Macrobiotic Way*, Avery, Wayne, 1985.

Belleme, Jan and John – *Cooking with Japanese Foods*, East West, Brookline, 1986.

Colbin, Annemarie – *Food and Healing*, Ballantine, New York, 1986.

Turner, Kristina – *The Self Healing Cookbook*, Earthtones, Grass Valley, 1987.

Aihara, Cornellia – *The Do of Cooking*, George Ohsawa Macrobiotic Foundation, Oroville, 1982.

Estella, Mary – *Natural Foods Cookbook*, Japan Publications, Tokyo, 1985.

Miller, Saul and JoAnne – *Food for Thought*, Prentice Hall, Englewood Cliffs, 1979.

A complete catalog of macrobiotic books can be obtained from George Ohsawa Macrobiotic Foundation, 1511 Robinson Street, Oroville, California 95965, (916) 533-7702.

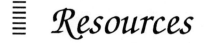 *Resources*

Live-In Macrobiotic Study Centers:

Vega Study Center, 1511 Robinson Street, Oroville, CA 95965;
(916) 533-7702.

Kushi Foundation, P.O. Box 7, Leland Road, Becket, MA 01223;
(413) 623-5742.

Mail Order Suppliers:

George Ohsawa Macrobiotic Foundation, 1511 Robinson Street, Oroville,
CA 95965; (916) 533-7702.

Gold Mine Natural Foods, 1947 30th Street, San Diego, CA 92102;
(619) 234-9711.

Granum, Inc., 2901 N.E. Blakeley Street, Seattle, WA 98105;
(206) 525-0051.

Mountain Ark Trading Company, 120 South East Avenue, Fayetteville,
AR 72701; (800) 643-8909.

Magazines:

East West Journal, P.O. Box 6769, Syracuse, NY 13217.

Macrobiotics Today, P.O. Box 426, Oroville, CA 95965.

Solstice/Macromuse, 201 East Main Street, Suite H, Charlottesville,
VA 22901.

Vegetarian Times, P.O. Box 570, Oak Park, IL 60303.

For information on macrobiotic activities in your area, contact George
Ohsawa Macrobiotic Foundation, 1511 Robinson Street, Oroville, CA
95965; (916) 533-7702.

☰ *Index*